How to Create Web Pages Using HTML
Brief Edition

Kenneth C. Laudon
Jason Eiseman

Azimuth Interactive, Inc.

Boston   Burr Ridge, IL   Dubuque, IA   Madison, WI   New York   San Francisco   St. Louis
Bangkok   Bogotá   Caracas   Lisbon   London   Madrid   Mexico City   Milan   New Delhi   Seoul
Singapore   Sydney   Taipei   Toronto

McGraw-Hill Higher Education

*A Division of The **McGraw-Hill** Companies*

1 2 3 4 5 6 7 8 9 0 QPD/QPD 9 0 9 8 7 6 5 4 3 2 1 0 9

ISBN   0-07-235856-4

Vice president/Editor-in-Chief: *Michael W. Junior*
Publisher: *David Kendric Brake*
Sponsoring editor: *Trisha O'Shea*
Associate editors: *Scott M. Hamilton/Steve Schuetz*
Developmental editor: *Erin Riley*
Senior marketing manager: *Jeff Parr*
Project manager: *Carrie Sestak*
Production supervisor: *Michael R. McCormick*
Freelance design coordinator: *Pam Verros*
Cover photograph: *© Wides & Holl/FPG*
Supplement coordinator: *Matthew Perry*
New media: *Lisa Ramos-Torrescan*
Compositor: *Azimuth Interactive, Inc.*
Typeface: *10/12 Sabon*
Printer: *Quebecor Printing Book Group/Dubuque*

Library of Congress Catalog Card Number: 99-067229

http://www.mhhe.com

How to Create Web Pages Using HTML
Brief Edition

Kenneth C. Laudon
Jason Eiseman

Azimuth Interactive, Inc.

At **McGraw-Hill Higher Education**, we publish instructional materials targeted at the higher education market. In an effort to expand the tools of higher learning, we publish texts, lab manuals, study guides, testing materials, software, and multimedia products.

At **Irwin/McGraw-Hill** (a division of McGraw-Hill Higher Education), we realize technology will continue to create new mediums for professors and students to manage resources and communicate information with one another. We strive to provide the most flexible and complete teaching and learning tools available and offer solutions to the changing world of teaching and learning.

Irwin/McGraw-Hill is dedicated to providing the tools necessary for today's instructors and students to navigate the world of Information Technology successfully.

Seminar Series - Irwin/McGraw-Hill's Technology Connection seminar series offered across the country every year, demonstrates the latest technology products and encourages collaboration among teaching professionals.

Osborne/McGraw-Hill - A division of the McGraw-Hill Companies known for its best-selling Internet titles *Harley Hahn's Internet & Web Yellow Pages* and the *Internet Complete Reference*, offers an additional resource for certification and has strategic publishing relationships with corporations such as Corel Corporation and America Online. For more information, visit Osborne at www.osborne.com.

Digital Solutions - Irwin/McGraw-Hill is committed to publishing Digital Solutions. Taking your course online doesn't have to be a solitary venture. Nor does it have to be a difficult one. We offer several solutions, which will let you enjoy all the benefits of having course material online. For more information, visit www.mhhe.com/solutions/index.mhtml.

Packaging Options - For more about our discount options, contact your local Irwin/McGraw-Hill Sales representative at 1-800-338-3987, or visit our Web site at www.mhhe.com/it.

Preface

How to Create Web Pages Using HTML

Approach

How to Create Web Pages Using HTML is a visual interactive way to develop and apply software skills. This skills-based approach coupled with its highly visual, two-page spread design allows the student to focus on a single skill without having to turn the page. A running case study is provided through the text, reinforcing the skills and giving a real-world focus to the learning process.

Each lesson is organized around Skills, Concepts, and Steps (Do It!).

- •Each lesson is divided into a number of Skills. Each Skill is first explained at the top of the page.

- •Each Concept is a concise description of why the skill is useful and where it is commonly used.

- •Each Step (Do It!) contains the instructions on how to complete the skill.

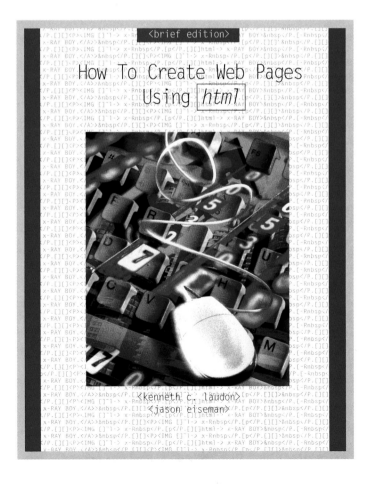

Using the Book

In the book, each skill is described in a two-page graphical spread (Figure 1). The left side of the two-page spread describes the skill, the concept, and the steps needed to perform the skill. The right side of the spread uses screen shots to show you how the screen should look at key stages.

Figure 1

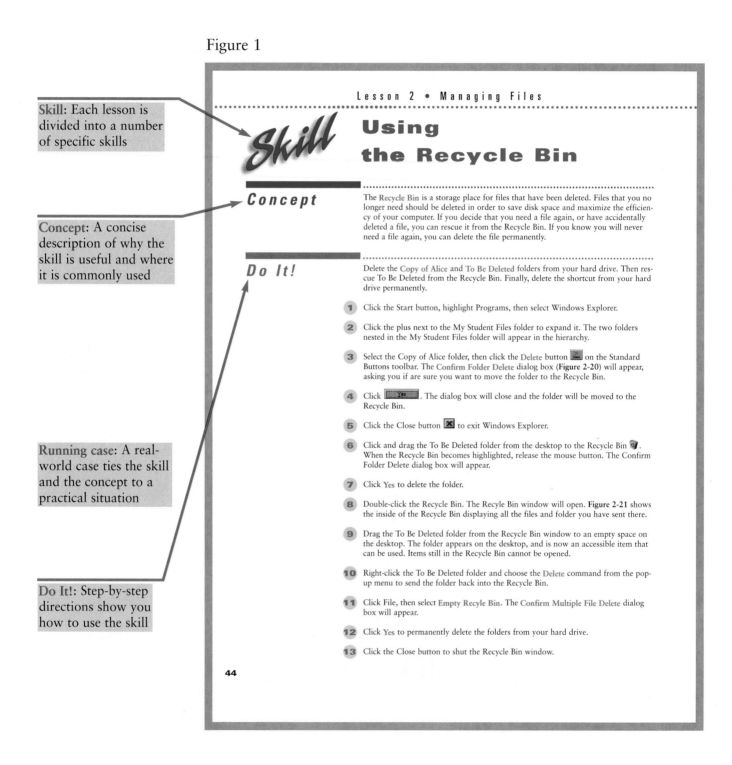

Skill: Each lesson is divided into a number of specific skills

Concept: A concise description of why the skill is useful and where it is commonly used

Running case: A real-world case ties the skill and the concept to a practical situation

Do It!: Step-by-step directions show you how to use the skill

---

Lesson 2 • Managing Files

Skill Using the Recycle Bin

Concept

The Recycle Bin is a storage place for files that have been deleted. Files that you no longer need should be deleted in order to save disk space and maximize the efficiency of your computer. If you decide that you need a file again, or have accidentally deleted a file, you can rescue it from the Recycle Bin. If you know you will never need a file again, you can delete the file permanently.

Do It!

Delete the Copy of Alice and To Be Deleted folders from your hard drive. Then rescue To Be Deleted from the Recycle Bin. Finally, delete the shortcut from your hard drive permanently.

1. Click the Start button, highlight Programs, then select Windows Explorer.

2. Click the plus next to the My Student Files folder to expand it. The two folders nested in the My Student Files folder will appear in the hierarchy.

3. Select the Copy of Alice folder, then click the Delete button 🗑 on the Standard Buttons toolbar. The Confirm Folder Delete dialog box (**Figure 2-20**) will appear, asking you if are sure you want to move the folder to the Recycle Bin.

4. Click ▭. The dialog box will close and the folder will be moved to the Recycle Bin.

5. Click the Close button ☒ to exit Windows Explorer.

6. Click and drag the To Be Deleted folder from the desktop to the Recycle Bin 🗑. When the Recycle Bin becomes highlighted, release the mouse button. The Confirm Folder Delete dialog box will appear.

7. Click Yes to delete the folder.

8. Double-click the Recycle Bin. The Recyle Bin window will open. **Figure 2-21** shows the inside of the Recycle Bin displaying all the files and folder you have sent there.

9. Drag the To Be Deleted folder from the Recycle Bin window to an empty space on the desktop. The folder appears on the desktop, and is now an accessible item that can be used. Items still in the Recycle Bin cannot be opened.

10. Right-click the To Be Deleted folder and choose the Delete command from the pop-up menu to send the folder back into the Recycle Bin.

11. Click File, then select Empty Recycle Bin. The Confirm Multiple File Delete dialog box will appear.

12. Click Yes to permanently delete the folders from your hard drive.

13. Click the Close button to shut the Recycle Bin window.

44

End-of-Lesson Features

In the book, the learning in each lesson is reinforced at the end by a quiz and a skills review called Interactivity, which provides step-by-step exercises and real-world problems for the students to solve independently.

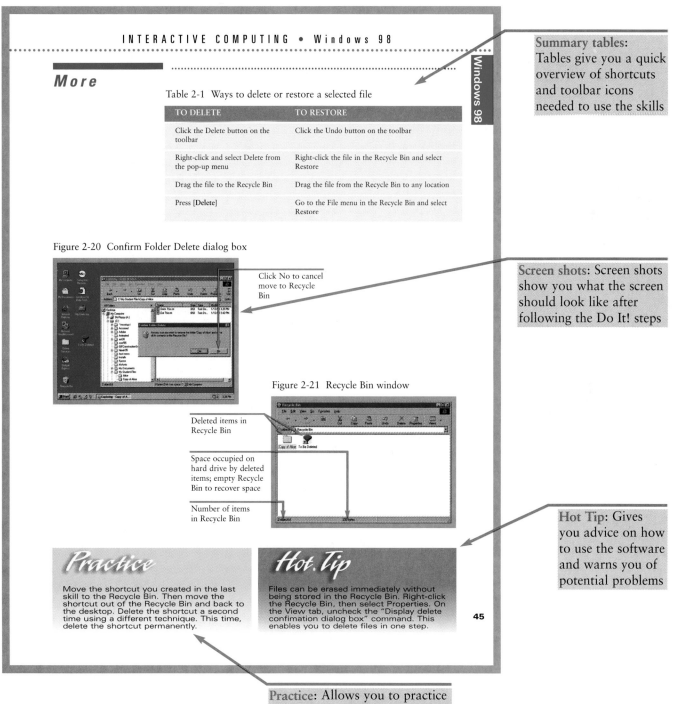

INTERACTIVE COMPUTING • Windows 98

Windows 98

More

Table 2-1 Ways to delete or restore a selected file

TO DELETE	TO RESTORE
Click the Delete button on the toolbar	Click the Undo button on the toolbar
Right-click and select Delete from the pop-up menu	Right-click the file in the Recycle Bin and select Restore
Drag the file to the Recycle Bin	Drag the file from the Recycle Bin to any location
Press [Delete]	Go to the File menu in the Recycle Bin and select Restore

Figure 2-20 Confirm Folder Delete dialog box

Click No to cancel move to Recycle Bin

Figure 2-21 Recycle Bin window

Deleted items in Recycle Bin

Space occupied on hard drive by deleted items; empty Recycle Bin to recover space

Number of items in Recycle Bin

Summary tables: Tables give you a quick overview of shortcuts and toolbar icons needed to use the skills

Screen shots: Screen shots show you what the screen should look like after following the Do It! steps

Hot Tip: Gives you advice on how to use the software and warns you of potential problems

Practice

Move the shortcut you created in the last skill to the Recycle Bin. Then move the shortcut out of the Recycle Bin and back to the desktop. Delete the shortcut a second time using a different technique. This time, delete the shortcut permanently.

Hot Tip

Files can be erased immediately without being stored in the Recycle Bin. Right-click the Recycle Bin, then select Properties. On the View tab, uncheck the "Display delete confimation dialog box" command. This enables you to delete files in one step.

45

Practice: Allows you to practice the skill with a built-in exercise or directs you to a student file

Teaching Resources

The following is a list of supplemental material available with the How to Create Web Pages Using HTML text.

Skills Assessment
Irwin/McGraw-Hill offers two innovative systems, ATLAS and SimNet, which take testing beyond the basics with pre- and post-assessment capabilities.
ATLAS (Active Testing and Learning Assessment Software) – available for all of our Microsoft Office applications – is our live-in-the-application Skills Assessment tool. ATLAS allows students to perform tasks while working live within the Office applications environment. ATLAS is web-enabled and customizable to meet the needs of your course. ATLAS is available for Office 2000.
SimNet (Simulated Network Assessment Product) – available for all of our Microsoft Office applications – permits you to test the actual software skills students learn about the Microsoft Office applications in a simulated environment. SimNet is web-enabled and is available for Office 97 and Office 2000.

Instructor's Resource Kits
The Instructor's Resource Kit provides professors with all of the ancillary material needed to teach a course. Irwin/McGraw-Hill is dedicated to providing instructors with the most effective instruction resources available. Many of these resources are available at our Information Technology Supersite www.mhhe.com/it. Our Instructor's Kits are available on CD-ROM and contain the following:

Diploma by Brownstone - is the most flexible, powerful, and easy-to-use computerized testing system available in higher education. The diploma system allows professors to create an Exam as a printed version, as a LAN-based Online version, and as an Internet version. Diploma includes grade book features, which automate the entire testing process.
Instructor's Manual - Includes:
-Solutions to all lessons and end-of-unit material
-Teaching Tips
-Teaching Strategies
-Additional exercises
PowerPoint Slides - NEW to the Interactive Computing Series, all of the figures from the application textbooks are available in PowerPoint slides for presentation purposes.
Student Data Files - To use the Interactive Computing Series, students must have Student Data Files to complete practice and test sessions. The instructor and students using this text in classes are granted the right to post the student files on any network or stand-alone computer, or to distribute the files on individual diskettes. The student files may be downloaded from our IT Supersite at www.mhhe.com/it.
Series Web Site - Available at www.mhhe.com/it.

Digital Solutions
Pageout Lite - is designed if you're just beginning to explore Web site options. Pageout Lite is great for posting your own material online. You may choose one of three templates, type in your material, and Pageout Lite instantly converts it to HTML.
Pageout - is our Course Web site Development Center. Pageout offers a Syllabus page, Web site address, Online Learning Center Content, online exercises and quizzes, gradebook, discussion board, an area for students to build their own Web pages, and all the features of Pageout Lite. For more information please visit the Pageout Web site at www.mhla.net/pageout.

OLC/Series Web Sites - Online Learning Centers (OLCs)/Series Sites are accessible through our Supersite at www.mhhe.com/it. Our Online Learning Centers/Series Sites provide pedagogical features and supplements for our titles online. Students can point and click their way to key terms, learning objectives, chapter overviews, PowerPoint slides, exercises, and Web links.

The McGraw-Hill Learning Architecture (MHLA) - is a complete course delivery system. MHLA gives professors ownership in the way digital content is presented to the class through online quizzing, student collaboration, course administration, and content management. For a walk-through of MHLA visit the MHLA Web site at www.mhla.net.

Packaging Options - For more about our discount options, contact your local Irwin/McGraw-Hill Sales representative at 1-800-338-3987 or visit our Web site at www.mhhe.com/it.

Visit www.mhhe.com/it
THE ONLY SITE WITH ALL YOUR CIT AND MIS NEEDS.

Acknowledgments

How to Create Web Pages Using HTML is a cooperative effort of many individuals, each contributing to an overall team effort. Our team is composed of instructional designers, writers, multimedia designers, graphic artists, and programmers. Our goal is to provide you and your instructor with the most powerful and enjoyable learning environment using both traditional text and new interactive multimedia techniques.

Our special thanks to Trisha O'Shea, our Editor for computer applications and concepts, and to Jodi McPherson, Marketing Director for Computer Information Systems. Both Trisha and Jodi have provided exceptional market awareness and understanding, along with enthusiasm and support for the project. They have inspired us all to work closely together. Steven Schuetz provided valuable technical review of all our interactive versions, and Charles Pelto contributed superb quality assurance. Thanks to our new publisher, David Brake, and Mike Junior, Vice-President and Editor-in-Chief. They have given us tremendous encouragement and the needed support to tackle seemingly impossible projects. Thanks to Robin Pickering, our developmental editor, for fine tuning our manuscripts for publication, ensuring that our ideas were accurately and clearly expressed.

The Azimuth team members who contributed to the textbooks and CD-ROM multimedia program are:

Ken Rosenblatt (Textbooks Project Manager and Writer)
Russell Polo (Chief Programmer)
Steven D. Pileggi (Interactive Project Manager)
Jason Eiseman (Technical Writer)
Michael Domis (Technical Writer)
Robin Pickering (Developmental Editor, Quality Assurance)
Raymond Wang (Multimedia Designer)
Michele Faranda (Textbook design and layout)
Stefon Westry (Multimedia Designer)
Caroline Kasterine (Multimedia Designer, Writer)
Tahir Khan (Multimedia Designer)
Joseph S. Gina (Multimedia Designer)
Irene A. Caruso (Multimedia Designer)
Josie Torlish (Quality Assurance)

Contents

Contents

Continued

Continued

L E S S O N

1

INTRODUCTION TO WEB PAGES

Designing Web pages is a creative adventure. You will need to use your creative instincts for color, text, images, and style in order to create useful and attractive Web pages. You will also need a good sense of organization because useful Web pages are well-organized collections of information.

HTML (Hypertext Markup Language) is a programming language used to create Web pages. You can use an ordinary word processor to create HTML documents that all Web browsers can understand and interpret. HTML may at first appear difficult to understand, but in fact it is a very simple language that you can learn in a few hours. The most difficult part of building useful Web pages is not learning HTML, but selecting the colors, text, images and other elements of Web pages.

Many people use graphical HTML editors such as Microsoft FrontPage, Adobe PageMill, or Macromedia's Dreamweaver to create Web pages without learning HTML. These graphical editors generate HTML code automatically based on your commands and instructions. However, it is quite often neccessary to edit the HTML produced by these programs. Also, you will be limited by the features provided by the programs. By learning HTML you will be able to edit and enhance the Web pages produced by these graphical programs.

In this book you will learn how to plan and organize a Web site; how to create HTML documents and Web pages; how to enter text and add graphics onto your Web pages, and how to create hyperlinks to other Web sites. Once you have mastered the basics, you will learn more advanced skills like creating forms and publishing Web pages.

Case Study:
Tom Randes is a freelance Web designer. Companies or individuals who want a professional Web site created but lack the technical expertise, hire a Web designer. Tom has just received an assignment from a company called Office Unbound, which specializes in organizing retreats and getaways in which management staff can bond in a nature setting. They have hired Tom to create a Web site for their business.

Skill

Introducing HTML

Concept

HTML, or Hypertext Markup Language, is a programming language used to create Web pages. Don't let the name scare you. While you will need to learn some simple commands, you don't need to become a computer programmer. All it takes to learn basic HTML is a few hours of reading and practicing.

HTML instructions, called tags, tell the Web browser what to display and how to display it. HTML tags describe the content of a document in detail. For example, tags tell the browser how to format text, what background color to use, and whether to display an image or a hyperlink.

HTML documents are plain text or ASCII files that are translated by programs called Web browsers to display the resulting Web page. They look like text scattered with greater than and less than symbols until you open them in a browser. HTML enables you to add rules, graphics, sound, and even video. HTML documents are saved in a text-only format that all computers can read and interpret.

HTML is an evolving language. In 1994 the World Wide Web Consortium (W3C) was founded to develop common standards for its development. However, in practice, competition between the two major browser manufacturers, Microsoft and Netscape Communications, compromise the universality of HTML. Each company creates new extensions to try to woo the Web surfing public to their product. Understanding how HTML works will enable you to stay abreast of the latest innovations. This knowledge will also help you decide what special effects to use based on how universal you want your page to be and who your intended audience is.

Many people never notice the HTML source page. When you surf the Internet you are viewing your Web browser's interpretation of an HTML source document. To view the source document, choose either View HTML Source or View Source from your browser's View menu. In fact this is one of the best ways to become familiar with HTML design principles. You can even download the source document, save it to your hard drive, reopen it in a basic text editor, enter your own content, and open the file in your Web browser to learn what that Web author did and how they did it. Copyright considerations cannot be ignored however, so use others' pages for inspiration and as a learning device only.

In this book you will learn how to structure and write the commands, or tags, used in HTML and how to use them to create Web pages to your specifications.

Figure 1-1 displays the HTML source for the National Oceanic and Atmospheric Association (NOAA)'s home page on the Internet. While it may look confusing to you now, it will not take long for you to learn which HTML commands are related to which graphical elements. If you look carefully you will notice that HTML is written in English, but uses abbreviations that are easy to learn and use.

Figure 1-2 is the same Web page shown in **Figure 1-1**, viewed through a Web browser. The HTML shown in **Figure 1-1** tells the browser to display the page seen in **Figure 1-2**.

Figure 1-1 HTML source of NOAA home page

Tags

HTML

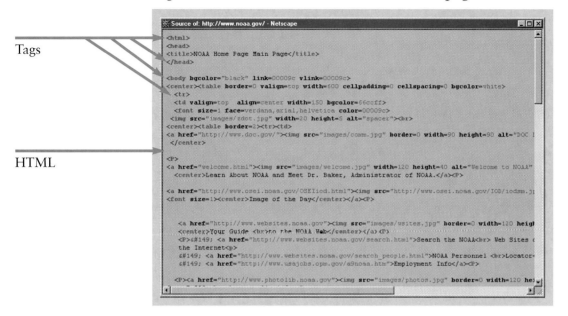

Figure 1-2 NOAA home page, as displayed by a Web browser

Graphic

Hyperlink

Formatted text

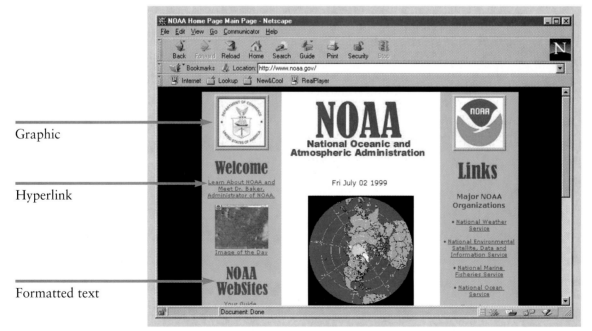

 # Introduction to Web Browsers

Concept

A Web browser is a computer program that interprets the commands found in HTML documents and converts those commands into a properly formatted Web page that appears on your screen. A very powerful feature of HTML and Web browser programs is that they are multi-platform. For instance, an HTML document on a Windows personal computer will appear nearly identical when displayed on a Macintosh personal computer or a Unix workstation. This means that no matter what type of personal computer you have, or where in the world you are located, you can use the Web. That's why it is called "The World Wide Web."

There are however slight differences among major brands of browers. The two market-leading browsers are Microsoft's Internet Explorer and Netscape's Navigator browser. Each company has given their browser programs proprietary extensions or capabilities not shared by the other. This produces slight differences in Web page display. Therefore, when you are designing Web pages you should have a copy of both major browsers to test your pages and ensure they display properly.

It is also wise to consider that not everyone in the world will have a high-speed modem connection, or a fast computer. In fact much of the world is still using older 486 computers with older operating systems that have difficulty displaying graphics. When designing your Web pages you may want to keep them simple and rely more on text in order to achieve the largest possible audience.

Figure 1-3 shows you the NOAA page again, viewed in the Netscape Navigator browser. **Figure 1-4** shows the same page viewed through the Internet Explorer browser. The HTML source document for the page is the same, but different browsers may interpret it differently.

In the case of the NOAA home page, the page looks almost the same in both browsers because the page was specifically designed to work with both Netscape Navigator and Internet Explorer. Another browser may not be able to display some of the fonts or images, or some of the other elements that are included in the page.

Figure 1-3 NOAA home page viewed in Netscape Navigator

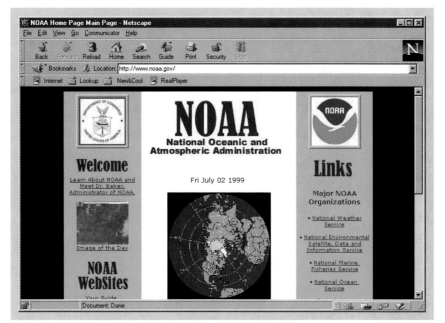

Figure 1-4 NOAA home page viewed in Microsoft Internet Explorer

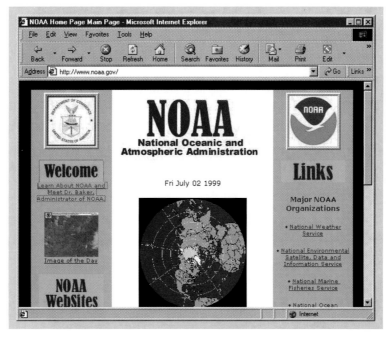

Skill   Using a Text Editor

Concept

You can create an HTML document using any text editor. A text editor is a simple word processing program. Using these free tools that come with your operating system, you can write HTML and save it in ASCII or plain text format to produce Web pages. For the exercises in this book we will use the text editor, Notepad, which comes with Microsoft Windows.

Do It!

Tom will open the text editor Notepad from Microsoft Windows.

1. Click **Start** on the Windows taskbar. The Start menu appears.

2. Move the mouse pointer over the Start menu to highlight Programs. The Programs submenu appears.

3. Move the mouse pointer over Accessories. The Accessories submenu appears.

4. Move the mouse pointer over Notepad, as shown in **Figure 1-5**. (Because the Windows Desktop is customizable, yours may not look exactly like the one shown in **Figure 1-5**.) Click the left mouse button.

5. The **Notepad** program opens, as shown in **Figure 1-6**.

More

Click the left mouse button once unless otherwise indicated. You may also be instructed to right-click (click the right mouse button once) or double-click (click the left mouse button twice in rapid succession.)

Notepad opens to a blank document. You will see a flashing black line called the insertion point. The insertion point tells you where the text will appear when you begin typing. You can move the insertion point (and thus the place where text will appear) by pressing the Spacebar or the Enter key.

Figure 1-5 Windows Desktop

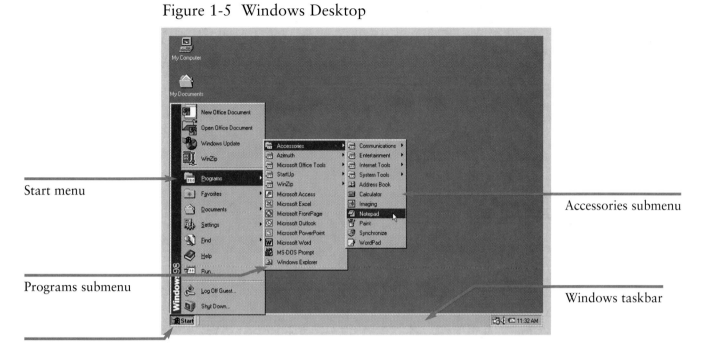

Start menu

Programs submenu

Start button

Accessories submenu

Windows taskbar

Figure 1-6 Notepad screen

Title bar

Menu bar

Blank page

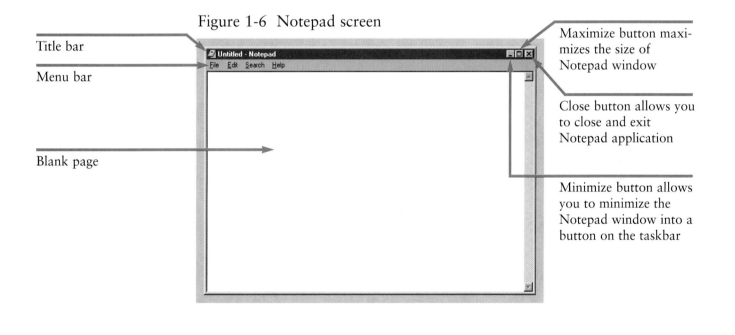

Maximize button maximizes the size of Notepad window

Close button allows you to close and exit Notepad application

Minimize button allows you to minimize the Notepad window into a button on the taskbar

Hot Tip

Other text editors you can use to write HTML are **Wordpad** for Windows, **Pico** for Unix, or **TeachText** for Macs.

Opening a Document and Viewing HTML Page Structure

Concept

All HTML pages adhere to a basic structure. You should learn this basic structure before you try to write HTML tags or commands. You must also know how to open a document written in a text editor, so that you can open HTML documents that you are working on.

Do It!

Tom will open an HTML document in Notepad and view the basic HTML page structure that every Web page includes.

1 Open Notepad on your desktop.

2 Click File on the Menu bar. The File menu opens.

3 Click Open on the File menu. The Open dialog box opens.

4 Click the drop-down arrow in the Look in: drop-down list box to locate the Student Files folder, as shown in **Figure 1-7**. Once you have located it, double click it. The contents of the file will be displayed.

5 Click on Doit1-3 to highlight it. Click Open. The file is opened in Notepad, as shown in **Figure 1-8**.

6 **Figure 1-8** shows the basic structure of an HTML page.

More

Every HTML page starts and ends with HTML tags. These tags indicate to the browser that an HTML source document will follow. The Head tag tells the browser that what immediately follows is the heading section of the document. The page's heading, or title, will appear in the browser's Title bar, and thus in any bookmarks or favorites folders and in search engine listings. You can also place messages and headers in this area. The first Body tag designates the beginning of the actual content. All text and page elements will be enclosed in the Body tags.

Figure 1-7 Open dialog box

Drop-down arrow

Drop-down
box

Allows you to view
a previous folder in
the folder hierarchy

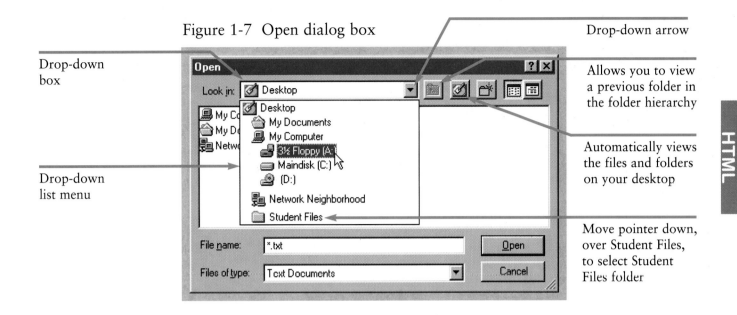

Drop-down
list menu

Automatically views
the files and folders
on your desktop

Move pointer down,
over Student Files,
to select Student
Files folder

HTML

Figure 1-8 Basic structure of HTML page in Notepad

HTML page
structure

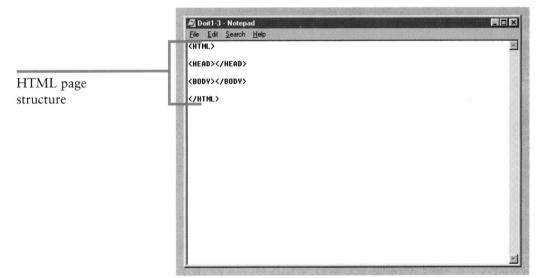

Understanding Tags

Concept

Tags are commands in HTML that are written between angle brackets: < >. A tag is written like this: <TAG>. Tags instruct a browser to display page elements in a certain way. Most tags require an opening tag and a closing tag to execute the command properly. An opening tag is written as <TAG>. A closing tag is written as </TAG>. The closing tag contains a backslash, /. Text contained outside the opening and closing tags will not be affected by the commands. Tags should be written in capital letters, if for no other reason than to differentiate them from the rest of the text. You can write tags in capital letters by holding the Shift key while pressing letter keys, or by pressing the Caps Lock key, and typing normally.

Figure 1-9 displays the basic HTML page structure we viewed earlier. Notice the opening tag, <HTML>. This tag indicates that what follows will be in HTML. The final line, </HTML>, designates the end of the page.

Text on a page may be affected by more than one set of tags.. For example, the opening body tag, <BODY>, and closing Body tag, </BODY> are contained within the HTML tags. Therefore all text contained within the Body tags is affected by both the body commands and the HTML commands. When we begin to add more specific commands, the text will be affected by all tags in which it is enclosed. **Figure 1-10**, the HTML source for the National Aeronautics and Space Administration (NASA) home page, illustrates the use of multiple tags. As a rule, all tags that appear within another set of tags should close within that set, as follows: <A><B>text</B></A>.

Tags may also include commands called attributes. Attributes affect specific features of a page such as background color, font, or the size of an object. Tags with attributes are written like this: <TAG ATTRIBUTE>. You can add as many attributes as you desire. The use of attributes is also illustrated in **Figure 1-10**.

Finally, when you write tags with attributes, you will have to specify values. Values indicate how an attribute should appear. For example, when you create a table you will have to specify the border thickness of the table, and the color of text. A value can be a number, color, or any other type of information. Values are generally enclosed in quotation marks, as follows: <TAG ATTRIBUTE="VALUE">. **Figure 1-10** also illustrates the use of values.

Some browsers change tags, attributes, and values to different colors, so you can differentiate them when you view the HTML source page, also as shown in **Figure 1-10**.

HTML browsers do not automatically add the spaces you insert in the source document into your Web page. Adding spaces and returns while you design and edit your HTML source document helps to maintain clarity, but do not use them to format the Web page. For example, if we added text between the Head and Body tags in **Figure 1-9**, the sentences would not appear on separate lines on the Web page. Instead, they would appear consecutively. Commands must be added to create paragraphs, spaces, and line breaks.

Figure 1-9 Basic HTML page structure

Opening tag

Closing tag

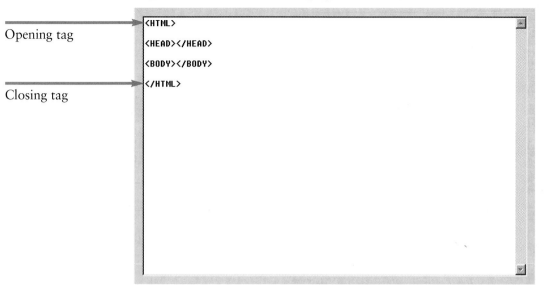

```
<HTML>

<HEAD></HEAD>

<BODY></BODY>

</HTML>
```

HTML

Figure 1-10 HTML source for NASA home page

Body tag marks the
opening of the body
of the page

Tag

Attribute

Value

Tag, attribute, and
value displayed in
different colors

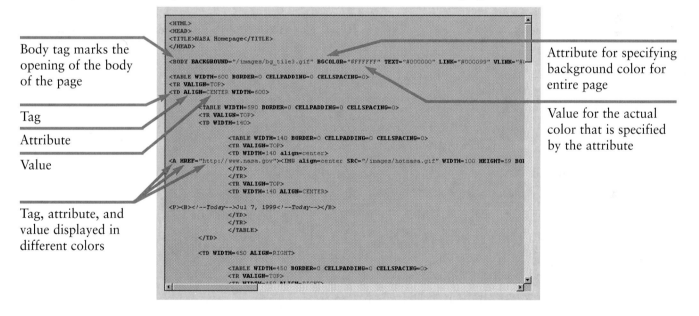

Attribute for specifying
background color for
entire page

Value for the actual
color that is specified
by the attribute

Practice

View a Web page in your browser. Then
view the HTML source of the page. This
can be done by selecting HTML Source,
Page Source, or View Source from your
browser's View Menu. Identify the **tags**,
values, and **attributes** in the **HTML** source.

Hot Tip

Certain tags automatically create new lines
or spaces on a Web page. For example, the
Header tag automatically includes a line
break, and the List Item tag
automatically creates a new line for each
line of text.

Writing Tags and Editing HTML Pages

Concept

Now that you are familiar with the concept behind tags, attributes and values, it is time for you to begin writing basic tags. It will take time and patience at first while you learn the common symbols, such as the backslash and the angle brackets, which comprise HTML code. After you learn these basic tags, you will be ready to move on to more complex tags.

Do It!

Tom is going to begin to create a Web page in HTML. He will start by creating some of the basic tags that every Web page requires.

1. Open the Notepad program. It should open to a blank page with a blinking insertion point in the top-left corner of the workspace.

2. Hold the Shift key on your keyboard and press the [,] key at the same time.

3. Type: HTML. Then hold the Shift key again and press the [.] at the same time.

4. Press the Enter key twice

5. Using the same method as above, type <BODY>. Press the Enter key again.

6. Type: </BODY>. Press the Enter key twice.

7. Type: </HTML>. Your page should now look like **Figure 1-11**. Notice that if you move the pointer around on the page it will turn into an I-Beam ⌶. Move the I-Beam in between the opening HTML tag and the opening Body tag and click. The insertion point is now where you clicked the I-beam. Press the Enter key.

8. Type: <HEAD>, and press the Enter key.

9. Type: </HEAD>. Your page should now look like **Figure 1-12**.

More

Even though browsers do not recognize them, it is advisable to add plenty of spaces to your HTML source document, especially the first few times you design a Web page. This will keep you from confusing different tags or improperly writing tags so that a browser will be unable to read them. The extra spaces will not affect the appearance of the Web page, but will keep your work clear and understandable.

To edit your HTML document, place the insertion point behind text that you want to delete. Then press the Delete key on the keyboard, or press the Backspace key. You can also double-click on the text to highlight it. Once the text is highlighted, you can press the Delete, Backspace, or Enter key to delete the text, or simply begin typing to replace it.

Figure 1-11 Basic HTML tags

Opening tags

Closing tags

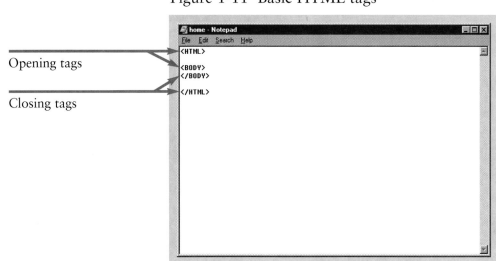

HTML

Figure 1-12 Basic HTML page structure

Head tag marks
the Head section
of the page

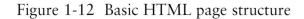
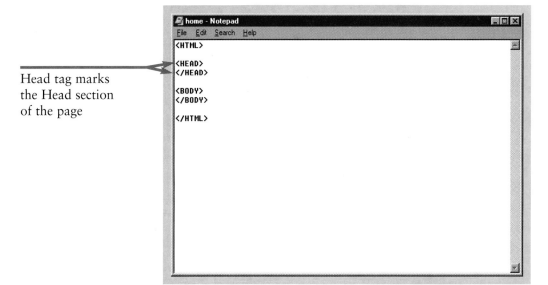

Practice

Open **Notepad** and create an HTML page structure identical to the one in **Prac1-5**.

Hot Tip

When you have a problem with an element not appearing correctly on your page, it is usually caused by a tag error. Sometimes a closing tag is omitted, or it does not have a backslash to identify it as a closing tag.

Skill Saving Pages

Concept

A crucial part of working with any computer-generated document, including HTML source documents, is saving your work. Although a simple Web page can be written in a few hours, more complex pages will take considerably longer to design. You will need to know how to save your document and how to select the correct format in which to save it. Periodically saving your work while you are composing is always prudent to prevent data loss in the event of a power outage or computer failure.

Do It!

Tom wants to save the HTML source document he has created.

1. Open Notepad.

2. Open the file Doit1-3.

3. Click File on the Menu bar.

4. Click Save As. The Save As dialog box opens.

5. Click the Desktop button 🗹 on the top-right of the dialog box.

6. Double-click in the File name: text box. Type home.

7. Your dialog box should look like **Figure 1-13**. Because the desktop is customizable, your dialog box may not look exactly the same.

8. Click 【 Save 】.

9. Notice that the Title bar has changed to reflect the new name, as shown in **Figure 1-14**.

More

The Notepad document home now appears on your desktop with an icon, 🗒. You can open the document by going through the process we described earlier, or you can simply double-click on the icon representing the document you want to open.

The Save command and the Save As command perform different functions. The first time you save a document, either command will open the Save As dialog box. However, after you have named a file and saved it in a specific location, the Save command will simply overwrite the existing document. The Save As command will enable you to change the name and/or location of the document. It allows you to make changes to and save a document with a new name while maintaining the original file under the initial file name. Both commands are accessed from the File menu.

To create a Web page from an HTML document, type .html after the name of the page. For example, in the exercise above you would have typed home.html. This will save the document as a Web page. Once you have saved a document as a Web page, it will open in your browser no matter where you have saved it. The document will also have a Web page icon rather than a Notepad icon.

Figure 1-13 Save As dialog box

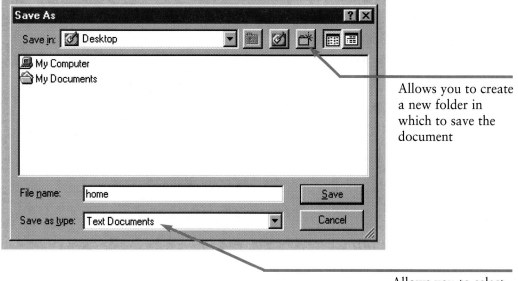

Allows you to create a new folder in which to save the document

Allows you to select the format in which a document is saved

HTML

Figure 1-14 HTML document after it has been saved

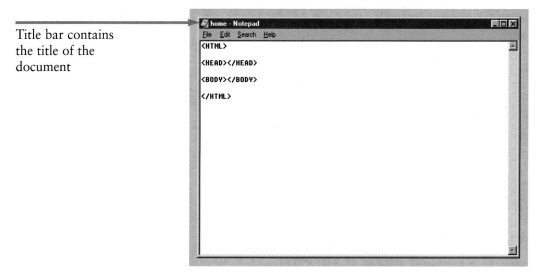

Title bar contains the title of the document

Practice

Open file **Prac1-5** in **Notepad**. Save it on your desktop as **Index**.

Hot Tip

Most home pages are titled either **home.html**, or **index.html**.

 # Printing an HTML Document

Concept

You may want to create a hard copy of the HTML document on which you are working. It is often easier to revise a printed document. You can make notes in the margins and correct tag errors that you may have missed on the screen. To do this, you must be able to print an HTML source document.

Do It!

Tom wants to print the HTML source document on which he has been working.

1. Open the home document in Notepad.

2. Click File on the Menu bar.

3. Click Page Setup. The Page Setup dialog box opens.

4. Make sure your Page Setup dialog box looks like **Figure 1-15**.

5. If there are differences between your Page Setup dialog box, make changes to resemble **Figure 1-15**.

6. Click Printer.... Another dialog box opens, as shown in **Figure 1-16**. Make sure the correct printer is selected.

7. Click OK. Then, click OK again.

8. Click File on the Menu bar. Then, click Print.

More

The Page Setup dialog box allows you to make changes to the way a document is printed. For example, you can change the page orientation from vertical to horizontal by clicking Landscape, or decrease the margins to ensure that a document will fit on one page. The options in the Page Setup dialog box will enable you to print information in the format you desire.

Figure 1-15 Page Setup dialog box

Specify paper size

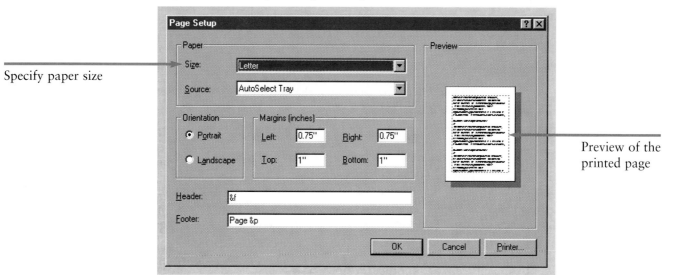

Preview of the printed page

HTML

Figure 1-16 Selecting a Printer

Name of the printer

Preview of the printed page

Practice

Print the **Index** page you saved earlier.

Hot Tip

Clicking [Printer...], then clicking [Properties] in the **Page Setup** dialog box allows you to select options, two-sided printing, increased color intensity and various font capabilities.

Skill

Planning a Web Site

Concept

Now that you are chafing at the bit to begin writing HTML documents and designing your own Web pages, you must take a step back and think carefully about the goals for your Web site. What do you want to accomplish?

Are you creating a business site or a personal forum for your own tastes and viewpoints? Planning your overall site organization, and the basic design and layout for individual pages, will save you time later. What information do you wish to convey? How many pages will you need and how will they be linked? What purpose will each page serve? Create an outline to answer these basic questions.

After you have decided how to link your pages within your site, you can consider links to other sites. For example, if you are creating a NASA resource page, you might consider linking to NASA's home page or another page on the site that complements the information you are providing. Create a list of URLs you are interested in and determine the optimum placement for each link.

Decide what objects and features you want to include in your Web site. You may want to add graphics, or use tables to organize information. You may want to insert multimedia files, or create a background sound. You may want to use a simple background color, or create a background image. There are many elements you can add to Web pages, but you must decide for yourself which ones are right for your Web site. You should also consider your audience at this point. Should you include lots of images, or is downloading time a concern? Is your intended audience likely to have the necessary hardware to view video or play sounds?

One of the best ways to plan your own Web site is to view other people's work. Surf the Web to get an idea of the possibilities. Note the different styles, elements, and organizational structures that appeal to you and those that you find distasteful. Visit sites with similar topics to see how they present the subject matter. Make a list of the elements you want to include. Finally, devise a simple, consistent set of names for your pages, images and other external files. Distinctive page and file names are important for both the Web site author and the Web site visitor. The Web author will need them to ensure accurate link construction and the visitor will require them for accurate site navigation.

Figure 1-17 shows how colors, links, objects, and multimedia files can be used in a Web page.

Figure 1-17 National Weather Service home page

Links within
Web site

Graphics and
multimedia
elements

Links to other,
related, Web sites

Shortcuts

Function	Opening Tag	Closing Tag
Signifies that the document is written in HTML	<HTML>	</HTML>
Signifies the beginning of the Web page	<HEAD>	</HEAD>
Signifies the body of the Web page	<BODY>	</BODY>
Tells the browser to display an attribute	<TAG ATTRIBUTE>	</TAG>
Tells the browser how to display that attribute	<TAG ATTRIBUTE="VALUE">	</TAG>

HTML

Identify Key Features

Name items indicated by callouts in Figure 1-18

Figure 1-18 HTML Source of National Weather Service Home Page

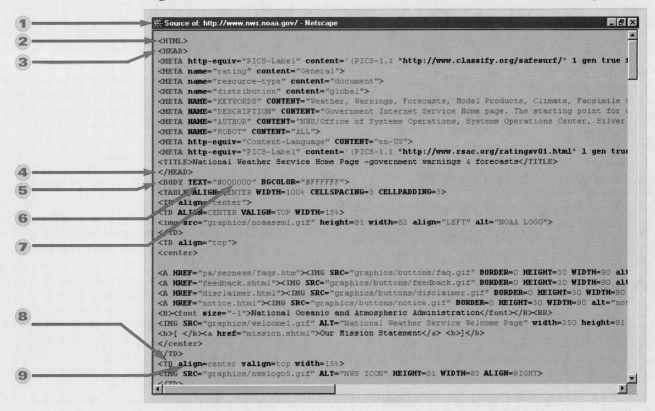

Select The Best Answer

10. A programming language used to design Web Pages

11. A document that appears on the Internet with its own URL

12. A simple word processing program

13. Commands written in HTML

14. A program that allows you to view Web pages

15. All text and page elements are contained within this HTML document section

16. Affects specific features of a tag

17. Specifies the way attributes should appear

18. Command that allows you to change the way a page will look when it is printed

a. Text editor

b. Web browser

c. Body

d. HTML

e. Attribute

f. Page Setup

g. Value

h. Web page

i. Tags

HT 1.21

Complete the Statement

19. Most tags require the following in order to execute a command properly:

    a. Message tags

    b. Opening and closing tags

    c. Capital letters

    d. Different colors

20. If you want to view the HTML source of Web pages on the Internet:

    a. You cannot because it is illegal

    b. You must first obtain permission

    c. You cannot because there is no way to view it

    d. You will discover one of the best ways to learn HTML

21. All of the following are text editors except:

    a. Notepad

    b. Wordpad

    c. TeachText

    d. HTMLpad

22. All of the following are part of writing HTML except:

    a. Linings

    b. Tags

    c. Attributes

    d. Values

23. The best way to get ideas for your own Web site is to:

    a. Poll as many people as possible

    b. View as many similar Web sites as possible

    c. Not let other Web sites influence you.

    d. Get someone to create it for you.

24. If you forget to add a closing tag, or make another syntax error:

    a. It will have no effect on your Web page

    b. A good text editor will correct the problem

    c. Your page will not display properly

    d. A browser will still read the HTML source correctly

25. The Save As command allows you to:

    a. Save the document under a new name and in a new location

    b. Save the document under the same name and in the same location

    c. Save the document under a new name but only in the same location

    d. Save the document in a new location but under the same name

26. You can make a page print horizontally by:

    a. Changing the paper size

    b. Changing the margins

    c. Changing the orientation to Portrait

    d. Changing the orientation to Landscape

Test Your Skills

1. Open a text editor:

   a. Click Start. Click Programs.

   b. Click Accessories. Click Notepad.

2. Open an HTML document:

   a. Click File. Click Open.

   b. Locate Student Files folder.

   c. Open Test 1 document.

3. Write tags:

   a. Click File. Click New. Do not save changes to Test 1.

   b. Type: <HTML>. Press Enter.

   c. Type: <HEAD></HEAD>. Press Enter.

   d. Type: <BODY></BODY>. Press Enter.

   e. Type: </HTML>.

4. Save an HTML document:

   a. Click File. Click Save As.

   b. Save document on your desktop as Web page.

5. Print an HTML document:

   a. Click File. Click Page Setup.

   b. Make sure the correct printer is selected.

   c. Close the Page Setup dialog box.

   d. Click File. Click Print.

HTML

Interactivity (continued)

Problem Solving

1. Congratulations! You have been hired as a Webmaster at The Fixit Company. The Fixit Company sells hardware to construction companies, private consumers, and hardware stores all over the country. The executives at The Fixit Company have decided that they want a Web site in order to reach more potential customers, and improve customer service. They have hired you to establish and maintain a Web site for their company. Your first duty is to come up with some ideas to show your new boss. Start by visiting hardware sites on the Internet. Make notes on how many pages the typical hardware site has, how they are linked, what functions the pages fulfill, and what graphics and multimedia elements are included. Note what elements you like and dislike. Record your findings. Outline the basic structure and functions you think will be useful and potentially profitable for the Fixit Company to prepare for a meeting with the executives. They have already requested a product ordering page, a page where consumers can check the status of their orders, and a "feedback/contact us" page. Include a product list page complete with product descriptions.

2. Begin by creating the basic structure for the first Web page. First, open a text editor. You may use Word Pad, Notepad or any other text editor installed on your computer. Type the basic tags to construct a template that you can expand upon later. Start with the <HTML> tag and include Head and Body tags. Save this rudimentary file as Fixit.

3. You must also bring a copy of this basic structure to your bosses at The Fixit Company. First open the Fixit page, if it is not open already, and print two copies. Make sure there is plenty of spacing in your document. If not, create spacing so that the document will be easier to understand. Also make sure all of your tags are written correctly. For example, make sure that every tag has an opening and a closing tag. If they do not, the page will not print properly.

4. Plan another Web site, not for corporate purposes, but rather as your own personal forum. Base the site on your interests and make an outline of your plans. You may want to focus on a particular sport, band or movie. Be creative and find a topic that really interests you. After you have decided on a topic, visit the Internet and search for similar sites. Again, note the elements you like and dislike, how many pages are in the site and how they are linked. You will use this plan to create your own Web site later on. Then create a template file with the basic structure of your Web site in your text editor, and save it as Personal.

Skills

L E S S O N

2

FORMATTING PAGES WITH HTML

In the previous lesson you learned how to plan your Web site and create the basic structure for your Web pages. Now it's time to start building your Web pages by adding text, images, and links to other pages. What really makes a Web page interesting and unique is the way in which the Web author formats its text, and places objects, images, and other elements on the page.

There are now approximately 800 million Web pages in existence. Besides being an incomparable information resource, the Internet is a showcase that enables people to display information in entertaining, amusing and artistic ways.

HTML offers Web authors the ability to include many sophisticated elements in their Web pages, such as titles, preformatted text, lists, tables, and hyperlinks. A hyperlink is an instruction that, when activated, links the user to a different Web page, either at the current site, or at another site. The ability to link Web pages together and allow users to move quickly from one Web site to another is one of the most important features of HTML.

In this lesson you will learn how to add titles, format text, and work with preformatted text. Next you will learn how to create paragraphs and insert line breaks. Then, you will learn how to add objects such as lists and tables and how to format them. Finally, you will learn how to create anchors and hyperlinks that allow users to move within HTML documents or to different Web sites.

Case Study:
Tom will now add and format text, and insert a list, a table, and hyperlinks in the Office Unbound Web page. He will expand the Web site by one page and link the two pages. The formatting options he employs will make the Office Unbound site more useful, attractive, and easier for other Web users to access and navigate.

Skill

Using Titles

Concept

Every HTML page should have a title. The title appears in the browser's Title bar. Search engines, bookmarks and favorites lists also use the page's title, so it should provide an accurate page description and perhaps a keyword, to increase the likelihood that Web surfers searching for that topic will find your page. The Title tags are placed inside the Head tags.

Do It!

Tom want to add a title to the home page.

1. Open the home document in Notepad.

2. Place the insertion point between the opening and closing Head tags.

3. Press the Enter key.

4. Type: <TITLE>.

5. Type: Office Unbound-A New Direction in Management Training.

6. Type: </TITLE>.

7. Press the Enter key.

8. Your document should look like **Figure 2-1**.

9. Click File on the Menu bar. Click Save.

10. Click File on the Menu bar. Click Save As. Save the document on your desktop as home.html.

11. The icon for your page will look different, depending on what default browser you have.

12. If you double-click on the home icon, your page will look like **Figure 2-2** in Netscape. It will look similar in Internet Explorer.

More

Titles are also listed in a browser's history list. When you surf the Web, each page you visit is logged in the history list. If your page does not have a title, there will be a blank space on the history list where the title should be.

If you simply write your title inside the Head tags, and do not enclose it in the Title tags, it will appear as text at the top of your Web page.

Figure 2-1 Title in an HTML document

Title tags are contained within the opening and closing Head tags

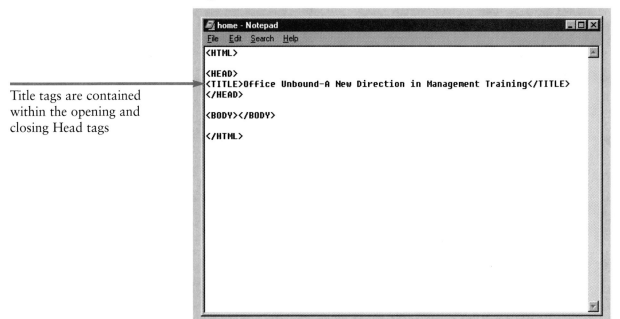

HTML

Figure 2-2 Title displayed in a Web browser

Title as it appears in a Web browser

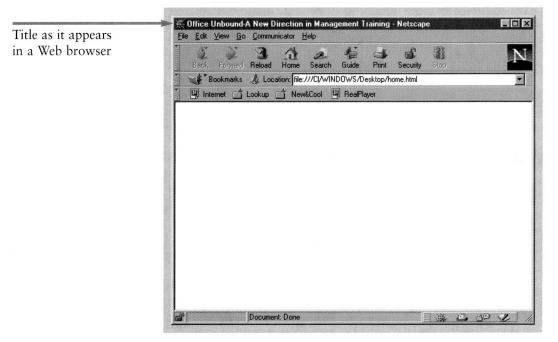

Practice

Add a title to the **Index** page you were working on earlier. The title should be **Don Knobley-Personal Accounting Firm**. Save the file.

Hot Tip

Pages can be displayed without a title, but they may display improperly and will not receive the benefits of being listed in favorite or bookmark folders, history lists or search engines.

 # Adding and Formatting Text

Concept

Text is usually the single most important element on a Web page. It can be used for a variety of reasons beyond the obvious ones of conveying information and communicating ideas. Text can be used to emphasize a point, enliven a page with color, or to clarify a table or form with a caption. It can even be used as an alternative to images for visitors with browsers that do not support graphics or who have slow connections. You can customize text to complement the style of your Web site.

Do It!

Tom will add text to the home page, and format it using a Header tag and italics.

1. Open the home document in Notepad.

2. Place the insertion point after the closing Title tag. Press the Enter key.

3. Type: <H1>Office Unbound.</H1>.

4. Place the insertion point between the opening and closing Body tags. Press the Enter key.

5. Type: <I>A survival retreat, where your management personnel can get to know each other, enjoy a natural setting together, and most importantly, learn to work together, as a team.</I>. Press the Enter key.

6. Your HTML document should look like **Figure 2-3**.

7. Click File on the Menu bar. Click Save.

8. Click File on the Menu bar. Click Save As. Save the file as home.html. Click [Yes] to replace the existing file.

9. When you open the home page in a browser it should look like **Figure 2-4**.

More

The <H> is a Header tag. It is an instruction to create a header in a certain preselected style. Instead of using specific tags to increase font size and make text bold, you can apply a Header tag. Headers are often used at the beginning of a page to construct a Table of Contents. There are 6 levels of Header tags. <H1> is the largest and most emphatic, and <H6> the smallest. It is not necessary to add attributes or values in order for browsers to interpret Header tags. However, remember that different browsers may display various modifications, so test your pages in several browsers to make sure you are satisfied with the results.

The <I> tag italicizes the enclosed text. Similar tags perform comparable functions. The Bold tag, <B>, for instance will make the enclosed text bold.

You can also use the tags <BIG> and <SMALL> to make text bigger or smaller relative to the surrounding text, without specifying an exact size value. Closing tags are required for all of the above tags.

Figure 2-3 Body text and a Header formatted in Notepad

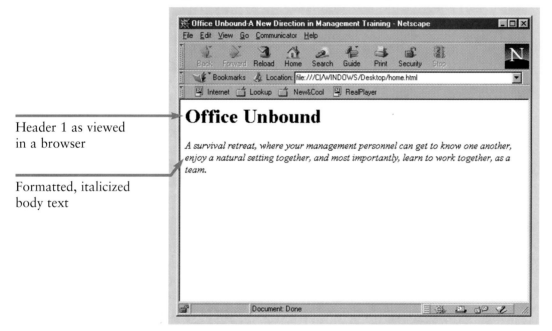

Header tag that formats
text in Header 1 style

Formatting tags
that italicize text

Body text contained
within formatting
tags

HTML

Figure 2-4 Home document displayed in a browser

Header 1 as viewed
in a browser

Formatted, italicized
body text

Practice

In the **Index** HTML document, create a Header, **Don Knobley**, in the **Header 2** format. Then, in bold, write **A Personal, Affordable, Accounting Firm** within Body tags. Save the document. Save it as an HTML Web page to view it in a browser.

Hot Tip

To change the font size, use the following a tag: **<FONT SIZE="#">**. The number should be between **1-7**, 7 being the largest font size, 1 being the smallest. Add a **+** or **-** to make the font size relative to the base font, and thus even larger or smaller.

 # Working with Preformatted Text

Concept

It is often difficult to guage exactly how your Web page will look on the Internet due to browser variables. Preformatted text enables you to display text in exactly the same layout as in your HTML source document. Your Web page retains the spacing and line breaks from the contained text in the HTML document. It is useful for designing simple tables and text graphics (ASCII art). The opening and closing tags for preformatted text are <PRE> and </PRE>.

Do It!

Tom will add preformatted text to his HTML document.

1. Open the home document in Notepad. Place the insertion point after the closing Italics tag in the last paragraph you wrote.

2. Press Enter twice.

3. Type: <PRE>Call. Press Enter.

4. Press Tab. Type the Underline tag, <U>, then type 1-800-555-4563.

5. Type the closing Underline tag, </U>. Press Enter.

6. Press Tab. Press Tab again. Type: to make an appointment today. Type: </PRE>. Press Enter. Your document should look like **Figure 2-5**.

7. Click File on the Menu bar. Click Save.

8. Click File on the Menu bar. Click Save As. Save the document as home.html. Click [Yes] to overwrite the previously saved document of the same name.

9. If you open the Web page, it should look like **Figure 2-6**.

More

In the next Skill you will learn how to write two commands that create space on your Web page without using preformatted text. Remember, normally when you add spaces and returns to your source document your browser does not recognize them. Only spacing that you add tags for will display. This is the major advantage of preformatted text. You can accurately space text on your source document and it will appear in exactly the same way in the browser.

You can add additional formatting to preformatted text as we did in the exercise above, but it is advisable to wait until after you have viewed the document in your browser. Tags take up space in the source document but not the Web page. You will want to have the spacing correct on the Web page and then determine how to insert the extra tags so as not to disrupt the page layout.

Although we applied underlining to the phone number in the exercise, you should be careful about applying underlining because it is commonly used to designate a link. You may confuse visitors who expect underlined text to be a hyperlink.

Figure 2-5 Preformatted text in an HTML document

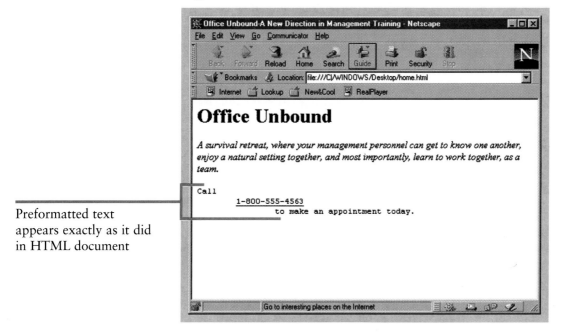

Preformatted
Text tag

Text contained
within Preformatted
Text tags

Preformatted
Text closing tag

HTML

Figure 2-6 Preformatted text in a browser

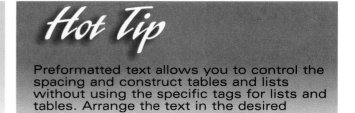

Preformatted text
appears exactly as it did
in HTML document

Practice

Create preformatted text below the bold text you entered earlier. Press Enter after each phrase you type. Type: **Low rates**, **Quick refunds**, **Knowledgable staff**, **In-house tax attorney**, and **Experience**.

Hot Tip

Preformatted text allows you to control the spacing and construct tables and lists without using the specific tags for lists and tables. Arrange the text in the desired format and enclose it in the <PRE> tags and all browsers will be able to read it.

Skill

Using Paragraphs and Line Breaks

Concept

Paragraphs can be created using the <P> tags, which break the text and insert a blank line. Line breaks can also be used to create space. The <BR> tags force a line break without inserting a blank line. Both tags start the text following the break on the left side of the page by default. The <BR> tag is useful for quotes or poems where you do not want the extra vertical space inserted. These two tags can help you to control the spacing of every element in your Web page.

Do It!

Tom will now add a paragraph and a line break to the home page.

1 Open the home document in Notepad.

2 Place the insertion point behind the closing Preformatted Text tag.

3 Press Enter twice.

4 Type: <P>"Our management crew was disorganized, and ineffective, but after the Office Unbound experience they're functioning as one big team."</P>.

5 Press Enter.

6 Type:
Nancy Villones</BR>. Press Enter.

7 Type:
CEO of Marthop Enterprises</BR>. Press Enter. Your document should look like **Figure 2-7**.

8 Click File on the Menu bar. Click Save.

9 Click File on the Menu bar. Click Save As.

10 Save the document as home.html. Click [Yes] to replace the previously saved file.

11 If you open the Web page in a browser, it should look like **Figure 2-8**.

More

Paragraph, Line Break, or Preformatted Text tags are necessary to create spacing in your Web page. If you add the same text as in the exercise but do not use the Paragraph, Line Break, or Preformatted Text tags, your Web page will look like **Figure 2-9**.

A closing Paragraph tag, </P>, is not necessary because once you have created a paragraph, you do not need to end it. You simply start another one. However, you may want to insert it anyway just to maintain the practice of typing opening and closing tags for every command. Furthermore when you advance to more complex procedures such as using Cascading Style sheets, you will need to close paragraphs to limit a font size, style, or color to that particular paragraph.

Figure 2-7 Paragraphs and spacing in an HTML document

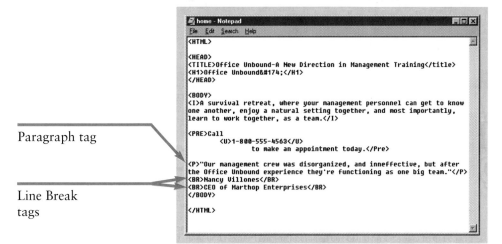

Paragraph tag

Line Break
tags

Figure 2-8 Paragraphs and line breaks displayed in a browser

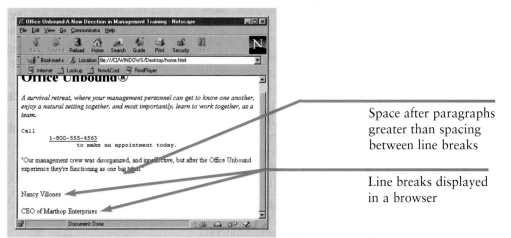

Space after paragraphs
greater than spacing
between line breaks

Line breaks displayed
in a browser

Figure 2-9 Spacing improperly displayed

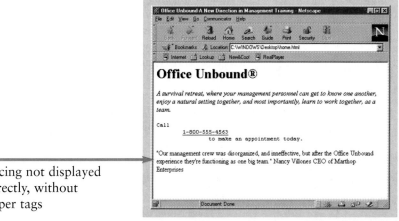

Spacing not displayed
correctly, without
proper tags

Practice

Add the following list to the **Index** document, with a line break between each line of text. The list is: **Established 1968, #1 Consumer Choice 5 Years in a row, Top Rated Accountant in the State**.

Hot Tip

Certain tags do not require you to create a new paragraph. For example, Header tags automatically include paragraph markers.

Skill Creating Lists

Concept

One of the most effective ways to organize information on a Web page is to create a list. HTML instructions include tags for creating several types of lists. You can create a list using preformatted text, but you have more control over the appearance of the list using the list commands. There are three types of lists: Ordered, Unordered and Definition. Ordered or numbered lists are generally used for outlines, sequential steps, or to prioritize information. Unordered or bulleted lists are the most common and are used for any series of items with no particular order. Definition lists are used for glossaries, or any list of words paired with a definition.

Do It!

Tom wants to add a list to another HTML document he has been working on.

1. Open the document Doit2-4, from your Student Files folder. It is the basic structure of an HTML document, with a lot of space between tags.

2. Place the insertion point one line below the opening Head tag.

3. Type: <TITLE>Advantages of a retreat with Office Unbound</TITLE>. Press Enter twice. Type: <H3>Advantages of a retreat with Office Unbound</H3>. Place the insrtion point one line below the opening Body tag.

4. Type: <UL>, the Unordered List tag. Press Enter.

5. Type: <LI>, the List Item tag. Then type: A feeling of comraderie</LI>. Press Enter.

6. Type the next items, pressing Enter after every entry. <LI>Learning to work together</LI>, <LI>Learning to lead a team</LI>, <LI>Learning to compromise</LI>, <LI>Building a common bond</LI>. Press Enter after the final entry.

7. Type: </UL>. Your document should look like **Figure 2-10**.

8. Click File on the Menu bar, then click Save As. Save the file on your desktop as advantage. Click File on the Menu bar, then click Save As. Save the file as advantage.html. If you open the Web page in your browser, it should look like **Figure 2-11**.

More

This is the most complicated tag we have learned thus far as it requires opening and closing tags and tags to mark each list item. The opening tags for an ordered list and a definition list are <OL> and <DL>, respectively. Use the <LI> tag to mark each list item in an ordered list just as you did in the unordered list in the exercise. In a Definition list, each list item is indicated by the tag <DT>, Definition Term, and each definition is tagged <DD>. Definition terms are neither numbered nor bulleted, but the definitions are indented.

HTML

Figure 2-10 Unordered list in an HTML document

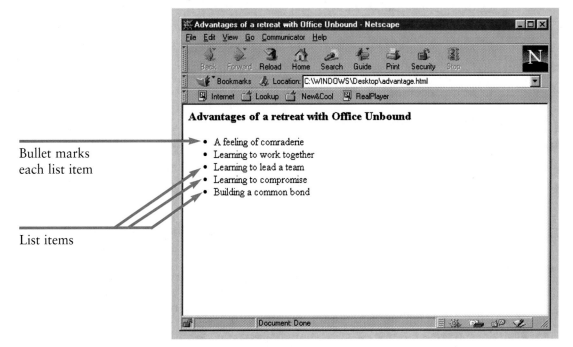

Specifies type
of list

List items

```
<HTML>

<HEAD>
<TITLE>Advantages of a retreat with Office Unbound</TITLE>

<H3>Advantages of a retreat with Office Unbound</H3>

</HEAD>


<BODY>
<UL>
<LI>A feeling of comraderie</LI>
<LI>Learning to work together</LI>
<LI>Learning to lead a team</LI>
<LI>Learning to compromise</LI>
<LI>Building a common bond</LI>
</UL>


</BODY>


</HTML>
```

Figure 2-11 Unordered list displayed in a browser

Bullet marks
each list item

List items

Advantages of a retreat with Office Unbound

- A feeling of comraderie
- Learning to work together
- Learning to lead a team
- Learning to compromise
- Building a common bond

Practice

Create a new document. Save it as **Top Ten**. Create a numbered list of the top ten reasons to see an accountant. Save the file.

Hot Tip

A **Nested list** is a "list within a list". Create the first list, place the pointer where you want the nested list to appear, and create it in the same way you created the regular list. For example, after **<LI>List Item</LI>**, type **<OL>** to create a nested ordered list.

HT 2.11

Skill Adding and Formatting Tables

Concept

Tables are commonly used in Web pages to organize information in a structured and attractive way. They consist of cells formed by the intersection of rows and columns. Creating a table is somewhat complicated because you must divide the information into rows and columns in the HTML source document. It also entails a number of steps, but a table is the perfect way to simplify complicated information. Tables can be created more easily using preformatted text, but you will not be able to add captions, borders, cell spacing or specific formatting to an entire row or column.

Do It!

Tom will create a table for the advantage page.

1. Open the advantage document in Notepad.

2. Place the insertion point one line below the closing Unordered List tag. Press Enter.

3. Type: <TABLE>. Press Enter. Type: <TR>, Table Row, to establish that the following items will appear in the same row. Press Enter.

4. Type: <TH>, the Table Header tag. Then type: Plans available:</TH>. Press Enter. Type: <TD>7 Day Plans</TD>. Press Enter. Type: <TD>5 Day Plans</TD>. Press Enter. Type: <TD>3 Day Plans</TD>. Press Enter. Type: <TD>Day Trips Available</TD>. Press Enter twice.

5. Type: <TR>. Press Enter. Type: <TH>Includes:</TH>. Press Enter. Type: <TD>Accomodations</TD>. Press Enter. Type: <TD>Fees</TD>. Press Enter. Type: <TD>Food</TD>. Press Enter. Type: <TD>The time of your life</TD>. Press Enter. Type: </TABLE>. Your table should look like **Figure 2-12**.

6. To create a border, place the insertion point inside the opening Table tag, after the word TABLE. Press the Space Bar. Type: BORDER. This is an attribute of the table.

7. Type: =3. This is the value for the attribute. It will tell the browser how to display the attribute. Your table should now look like **Figure 2-13**.

8. Click File on the Menu bar. Click Save. Click File on the Menu bar. Click Save As. Save the file as advantage.html. Click [Yes] to replace the existing file. If you open the Web page in a browser, it will look like **Figure 2-14**.

More

To place headers in the top row of the table, use a <TH> (Table Header) tag for each item you want to be a header. The <TD> tag is simply used to add cells to a table, the same way the List Item tag adds items to a list.

Border thickness is measured in pixels. The table border will be more pronounced as the value for the Border attribute increases.

Figure 2-12 Table created in an HTML document

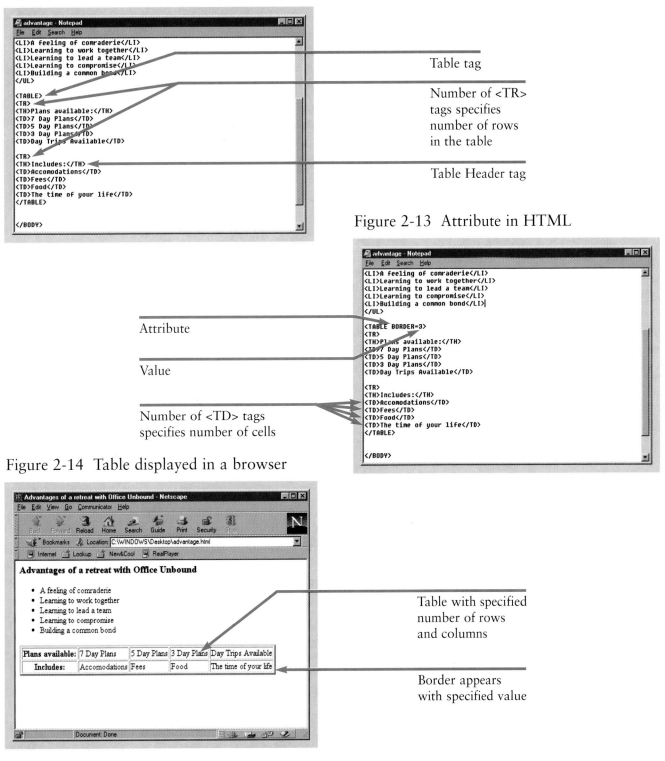

Table tag

Number of <TR>
tags specifies
number of rows
in the table

Table Header tag

Figure 2-13 Attribute in HTML

Attribute

Value

Number of <TD> tags
specifies number of cells

Figure 2-14 Table displayed in a browser

Table with specified
number of rows
and columns

Border appears
with specified value

HTML

Practice

In the **Index** page, add a table with three rows and columns. Add: **Don Knobly** in the first two cells of the first row. Then add: **452 Debonair Ave.** in the three cells in the second row. Then add: **Walker, R.I. 57068,** in the three cells in the third row.

Hot Tip

You can convert a table from Microsoft Word into an HTML table by selecting the **Convert Table to Text** command from the **Table** menu.

Skill Understanding Anchors

Concept

Links can be created to connect to a specific section of a Web page. For example, you can create a link from the top of a page to the bottom of a page. First you will need to create an anchor, which will be referenced when you construct the link. An anchor simply marks a location so that the browser will navigate to it. Anchors are particularly effective for use in lengthy documents. Each section can link back to the Table of Contents. Anchors can be used to construct links within the same document or to a particular area of another Web page. An anchor is created using <A> tags, and the Name attribute. The value for the Name attribute will be the name for the anchor.

Do It

Tom Randes wants to create an anchor and a link to that anchor in an HTML document he had worked on earlier.

1. Open the file Doit2-8 in Notepad.

2. Scroll down to the last paragraph, or List Item.

3. Place the insertion point after the <LI> tag.

4. Type: <A NAME=MOST>.

5. Place the insertion point at the end of the paragraph, contained within the closing List Item tag.

6. Type: </A>. This will make the entire paragraph the anchor.

7. Scroll up the screen and place the insertion point between the two Head tags.

8. Type: <A HREF=#MOST>Most Important Words</A>.

9. Click File. Click Save As. Save the file as tips. Your document should look like **Figure 2-15**.

10. Click File. Click Save As. Save the document as tips.html. Open the page in a browser. Your page should look like **Figure 2-16**.

11. When you move the pointer over the Most Important Words link, the text that is a different color, it turns into a hand, 🖑. If you click on the link, it will take you to the anchor, which is the final List Item.

More

The <A> tag informs the browser that you are creating a link. The HREF attribute stands for Hypertext Reference. If the anchor was in a separate document, such as page.html, you would type: <A HREF= "page.html#anchor name"> to reference the section.

Do not put quotes around a Name or HREF value unless the value contains more than one word. If you put quotes around a one-word value, the link will not function properly.

Figure 2-15 Link to an anchor in an HTML document

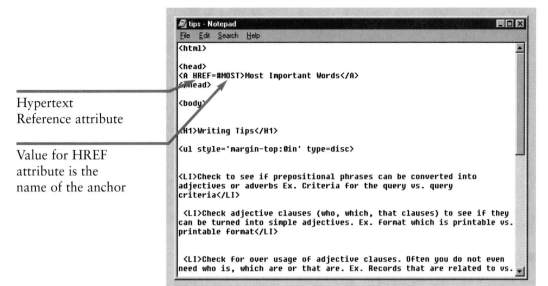

Hypertext
Reference attribute

Value for HREF
attribute is the
name of the anchor

Figure 2-16 Link to an anchor in a browser

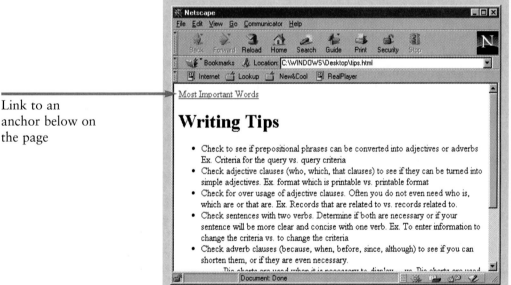

Link to an
anchor below on
the page

Practice

Create an anchor using the last List Item on the **Top Ten** page. Create a link to the anchor at the top of the page. Save the file.

Hot Tip

Some browsers use the term **target** and **anchor** synonymously. While they are similar, an **anchor** on a page is different from the **target** of a hyperlink. The term target will be further explained on the next page.

 **Creating Hyperlinks**

Concept

Hyperlinks are the essence of the World Wide Web. They are pieces of text or images that enable you to jump from page to page within a site or to pages on other sites. A hyperlink connects you to a target or destination document. While an anchor "bookmarks" a particular section of a Web page, a hyperlink connects to the top of the page. Hyperlinks can also be designed to download files, play an audio or video clip, or send e-mail. The value for a hyperlink is the Web page URL.

Do It!

Tom will create a hyperlink that links the home page to the advantage page.

1. Open the home document in Notepad.

2. Place the insertion point behind the closing Line Break tag at the bottom of the page.

3. Press Enter twice.

4. Type: <P><A HREF=advantage.html>Advantages of Coming to Office Unbound</A></P>.

5. Click File on the Menu bar. Click Save. The document should look like **Figure 2-17**.

6. Click File on the Menu bar. Click Save As. Save the document as home.html. Click [Yes] to replace the existing file.

7. Open the Web page in your browser. This page is shown in **Figure 2-18**. Scroll to the bottom of the page if neccessary.

8. Move the pointer over the hyperlink we created, so that it turns into a hand, 🖐.

9. Click on the hyperlink. You are connected to the advantage Web page.

More

The process is slightly different to link to another Web site. For example, if you wanted to create a link to the Web site www.domain.website.com, you would type: <A HREF="http://www.domain.website.com">HYPERLINK</A>. You can also substitute a protocol like ftp: if the address you are linking to does not use HyperText Transfer Protocol. Simply write the location of the address exactly as you would if you were telling your browser to open that page.

In the Do It! exercise above, we used a relative pathname to specify the location of the advantage.html file. A relative pathname is a "short-hand" way of specifying a file's location, but only works when the file being referenced is in the same folder as the current document. If it is not, you must use an absolute pathname, which specifies the exact location of the file with more precision. We will explain relative and absolute pathnames further in the next lesson.

Figure 2-17 Creating a hyperlink in an HTML document

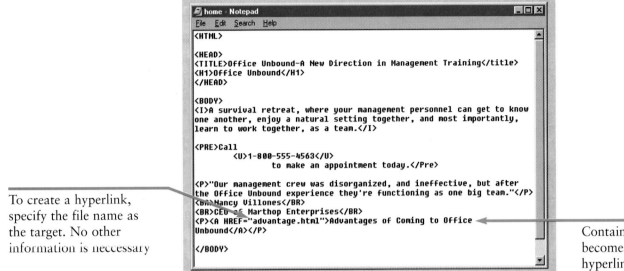

To create a hyperlink, specify the file name as the target. No other information is neccessary

Contained text becomes actual hyperlink

Figure 2-18 Hyperlink in a browser

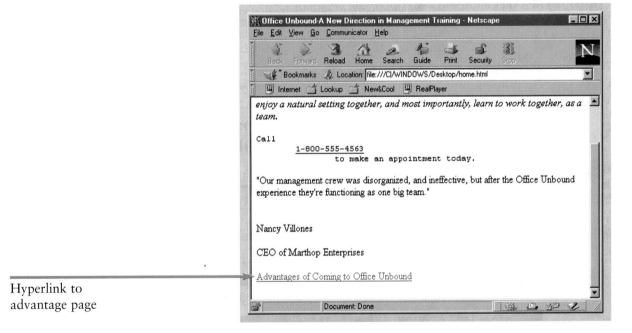

Hyperlink to advantage page

HTML

Practice

Create a link at the bottom of the **Index** page to the **Top Ten** page you created. Save the file, and make sure the hyperlink works by viewing the page in your browser.

Hot Tip

Every time you link, test the link in the browser to make sure that it works properly. Every link should work when it is clicked in your browser.

Skill Adding Colors to a Web Page

Concept

HTML allows you to add background color, and choose colors for text, hyperlinks, tables, borders and more. This enables you to create pages that are attractive and fun. You can set default colors for an entire page or add color individually to objects or text.

Do It!

Tom will add a background color and change the text color on the advantage Web page.

1. Open the advantage document in Notepad.

2. Place the insertion point between BODY and the closing angle bracket, >, in the <BODY> tag. Press the Space Bar.

3. Type: BGCOLOR="#FFFF10". BGCOLOR is the attribute for background color. The value is a Hexadecimal code for a shade of the color yellow. The Hexadecimal system will be explained below.

4. Press the Space Bar. Type: TEXT="#299C39". The value is coding for a shade of green. Your document should look like **Figure 2-19**.

5. Click File on the Menu bar. Click Save.

6. Click File on the Menu bar. Click Save As. Save the file as advantage.html. Click [Yes] to overwrite the existing file. Open the Web page in your browser. It should look like **Figure 2-20**.

More

Changing the color of text for a specific object such as a list or a table, or a section of text, is simple. Instead of the Text tag, use the Font tag, Color attribute, and a Hexadecimal value, as follows: <FONT COLOR="#######">. Then, add the closing tag, </FONT>. The text you want to change must be contained within these tags.

There are sixteen predefined colors. You do not have to use a Hexadecimal value to use these colors. You may simply use the name of the color. For example, if you wanted to set the default background to the color lime, type <BODY BGCOLOR="LIME">.

Th Hexadecimal system is a complicated way of creating colors on a Web page. The Hexadecimal system is based on the combination of Red, Blue, and Green that make up a particular color. First type #, then the Hexadecimal combination of six letters and numbers. Lighter colors generally have more letters, and typically begin with the letter F. For example, White is #FFFFFF. Darker colors usually contain more numbers. Black is #000000. Note that Black and White are predefined colors, so you do not need to know their Hexadecimal numbers to use them. In the appendices at the end of this book there is a reference guide that lists the names and color for the sixteen predefined colors and their attribute names. It also includes the Hexadecimal code for many common colors.

HTML

Figure 2-19 Color attributes and values in HTML

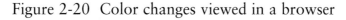

Attributes for setting the default color

Values specify the exact colors to be used

Figure 2-20 Color changes viewed in a browser

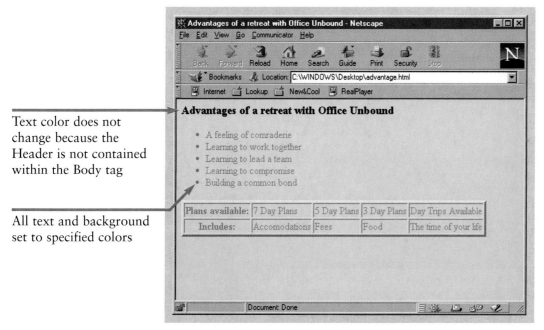

Text color does not change because the Header is not contained within the Body tag

All text and background set to specified colors

Practice

Change the background color on the **Top Ten** page to **black**, and make the default text color **white**.

Hot Tip

The Hexadecimal system uses sixteen symbols, **0-9** and **A-F**. These sixteen symbols specify the red, green, and blue components of 255 colors in a base 16 format.

HTML Tag	Appearance in Browser
<H1>	# Heading 1
<H2>	## Heading 2
<H3>	### Heading 3
<H4>	#### Heading 4
<H5>	##### Heading 5
<H6>	###### Heading 6

HTML

Identify Key Features

Name the items indicated by callouts in **Figure 2-21**

Figure 2-21   Advantage HTML document

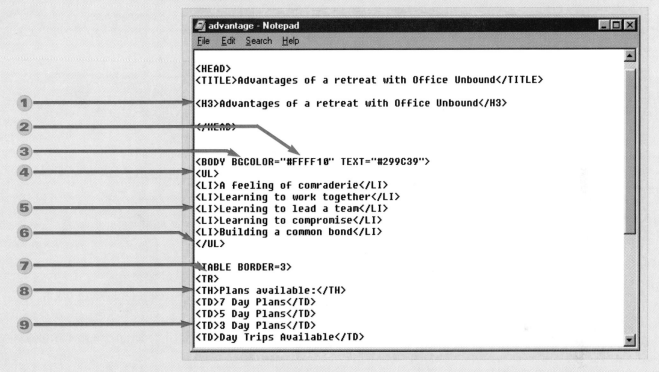

Select The Best Answer

10. Appears in the browser, but not in the Web page	a.
11. Text that will appear on a Web page as it appears in the HTML source	b. <DD>
12. Tag that identifies a line break	c. Hexadecimal
13. Tag that identifies a term definition	d. Title
14. Tag that identifies a table item	e. Anchor
15. A type of system used to add colors on a Web page	f. Preformatted
16. A location in pages of text that is marked and will later be linked to	g. <TD>
17. The destination of a hyperlink	h. Target

Complete the Statement

18. The Title tag is contained within these tags:

    a. Body

    b. Paragraph

    c. Head

    d. Table

19. You do not need to use Paragraph tags when you are using Header tags because:

    a. Header tags automatically create new paragraphs

    b. It will appear in the Web page exactly as it appears on the HTML document

    c. Every browser reads and displays HTML the same way

    d. Headers and paragraphs are interchangeable

20. If you want to create multiple paragraphs of text without a lot of space in between:

    a. Use the Paragraph tag

    b. Use the Header tag

    c. Use the Ordered list tag

    d. Use the Line break tag

21. An Ordered list is also known as:

    a. A Bulleted list

    b. A Numbered list

    c. A Definition list

    d. A To Do list

22. A way of marking text in a document so it can be linked to:

    a. Anchor

    b. Target

    c. Hyperlink

    d. Superlink

23. To add color to a specific piece of text on a Web page, use:

    a. <Text="######">

    b. <TXTCOLOR="######">

    c. <FONT COLOR="######">

    d. <WORD COLOR="######">

24. To add color to a Web page:

    a. Use the name of the color and the shade, light or dark

    b. Use the Hexadecimal code for the specific color you want

    c. Use one of the 31 predefined colors

    d. Use the tag <COLOR>

25. The tag <TR> stands for:

    a. Tall Roof, for large borders in a table

    b. Target Right, for use with hyperlinks

    c. Tree, to place a tree diagram on the Web page

    d. Table Row, to add a row to a table

Test Your Skills

1. Add a title and text to a document:

   a. Open the document Web page in Notepad.

   b. Add a title to the Head section of the document. The title is Sunglass City.

   c. In the Body section of the text, add a Header 3. The Header also reads Sunglass City.

   d. Use the BIG tag to format a paragraph of text on your page. The paragraph is Sunglass City-Where the days are hot and the glasses hotter.

   e. Click File. Click Save As. Save the document as sunglass.

2. Add preformatted text to a Web page:

   a. Add this preformatted text to the sunglass document. Press Enter after each piece of text: Low prices; Huge selection; Discounts; Medical plans accepted; Convenient location.

3. Create a list:

   a. Add an Unordered list to the sunglass page.

   b. The list items are: Gargantuas; Tree frogs; Apple eyes; Rose colored; Hunky Dorey; and many others.

4. Create a table:

   a. Create a new HTML document in Notepad, beginning with the basic HTML structure. Save the page as prices.

   b. Create a table on the prices page. Make sure the table has a border size of 7.

   c. Create three rows, with three Headers. The Headers will be Price range for the first row, Styles for the second row, and Availability for the third row.

   d. The first row will have four table items: $10-25; $30-50; $60-90; and 100 and over.

   e. The second row will have four table items: Mens; Womens; Childrens; and Prescriptions.

   f. The third row will have only one table item: All styles subject to availability.

5. Create a hyperlink:

   a. Add a hyperlink to the prices page. The hyperlink will appear in the Head of the document.

   b. Make the link from the prices page to the sunglass page.

6. Add color to a Web page:

   a. Change the background color of the sunglass page and the prices page to white.

   b. Change the color of the data in the table on the prices page to a shade of blue, using this Hexadecimal code: #00A5C6.

HTML

HT 2.23

Interactivity (continued)

Problem Solving

1. It's time for you to start working on a Web site for The Fixit Company. Open the Fixit document you created earlier. First add the title to the page. Create a Header on the page that also says The Fixit Company. You should also include the slogan of the company: Heavy on selection, light on the wallet. Create the following paragraph and format it in bold: We are one of the largest distributers of hardware equipment in the United States, selling to retail outlets, construction companies, and private consumers. Use preformatted text to create a list of locations, pressing Enter after each location: Boston, Chicago, Kansas City, Miami, Seattle, San Diego, Houston, and Charlotte. Save the file.

2. Create a new document in Notepad, beginning with the basic HTML structure. Save the page as Options. First title the page, The Fixit Company-Payment Options. Then create a Header, Payment Options. Then create a list of payment options. You can use whatever list you think works best. The list items are: Cash, Credit, Cash on delivery, Check, Money order, and Debit. Next, create a table. The table will have two rows. The Header for the first row will be Amount spent, the Header for the second row will be Shipping charge. The table items for the first row are: Less than $100, $101-250, $251-500, $500-$1000. The table items in the second row are: $15, $35, $70, and $150. Below the table create a new paragraph that says: Over $1000 dollars must be special ordered, from 1-800-555-5613. Create one hyperlink from the Fixit page to the Options page, then create another hyperlink from the Options page to the Fixit page. Add colors to both pages. Use the references at the end of this book to choose colors for the text and background of these pages. Save the file.

3. Begin creating your own personal Web site. Open the document you saved earlier as Personal. Create a title for the document that denotes the subject of the page. For example, if you created a soccer Web site you might title it The Your Name Soccer Page, or something to that effect. You may want to create a header, although it is not required. Write a paragraph describing the Web site; its purpose, some personal information about yourself, such as your age, where you live, and your education. Format the text in any way you see fit. You may use the formatting tags we used earlier, or preformatted text. Save the file.

4. Finally, create another page in your personal Web site. Call this new page Index. First create a hyperlnk that connects from the Index page to your Personal page. Then create a hyperlink that connects from your Personal page to the Index page. Make a list on the Index page. The list can be of anything related to your topic. For example, if you created a Web site devoted to movies you might want to list your ten favorite movies. Then, make a table. A table does not have to have Headers; you can simply use them to organize information in an attractive way. Finally, add color to your Web pages. Save both pages.

L E S S O N

3

ADVANCED HTML FEATURES

You now know the basic principles of HTML, and how to enter and format text, and create anchors and hyperlinks. Congratulations! Now its time to add the sizzle– graphics, images, and other elements that can make a Web page beautiful and exciting.

In this lesson, you will learn how to insert and format images and how to wrap text around them. You will also learn how to create an image map and how to work with multimedia files including sound, animation, and video. These elements will allow you to begin using your creativity to stamp your Web page with your own unique style.

Next, you will learn how to apply character tags (which enable you to format just a few characters or a few words) and how to code for special characters. Special characters are unusual symbols, foreign language letters, and accents that are not found on a standard keyboard. Finally, you will learn how to create an e-mail link and how to use pathnames.

You will also learn to work with tags that require multiple attributes and values. This might be confusing at first, but once you become familiar with the technique, the process will become clear.

The skills that teach you how to add beautiful and exciting elements are somewhat difficult, but will be worth the effort when you are designing sensational Web pages!

Case Study:
Tom wants to use some advanced HTML formatting options to enhance the appearance of his Web page. He is almost finished completing the project, and is making some final changes.

Skill

Introduction to Web Page Graphics

Concept

Text-only pages are not going to capture the imagination of the Web surfing public. The best way to add some pizzazz to your pages is to insert images. Images can display or explain information in a lively eye-catching manner.

Adding images is fairly easy. The tag is <IMG SRC="file">. The source attribute simply designates the location of the image. The HTML image formatting options are slightly more difficult to construct.

When you add an image to a Web page, it is not actually part of the document. The image tags tell the browser where to find the image and how to display it. For this reason, you must make sure that the image file name is correct, and that the image is located in the same folder or location as the Web page. This method of accessing an image is known as "inline." An inline image is displayed with a Web page. An external image, on the other hand, must be downloaded separately. Sometimes a miniature version or an icon serves as a hyperlink that leads the visitor to the full-size version.

The most important factor to consider when inserting images is file size. The larger a Web page is, the more memory it requires, and the longer it will take to download. Resist the temptation to add too many images, as each one will increase page-loading time. Several image formats reduce file size and are supported by most browsers.

Most browsers support Graphic Interchange Format (GIF). It is relatively small and is sufficient for low-resolution images. For larger, more color intensive images, the Joint Photographic Experts Group (JPEG) format should be used. Most browsers also support JPEG. GIF and JPEG are the two most common image formats used on the Internet. The GIF format is sufficient for logos, banners and other computer generated art. JPEG should be used for photographs and images with more than 256 colors.

Before you insert an image, you should format it in an image editor such as Adobe Photoshop, Image Edit, or Paint Shop Pro. Image editors allow you to resize, reduce the number of colors in, compress, and save images as JPEG or GIF files. These procedures will help keep download time to a minimum. Photographs can be saved using JPEG compression to retain satisfactory quality while achieving a file size that will not take forever to load.

In this lesson you will learn how to add an image to your Web page and how to apply some of the available formatting options. You will also learn how to turn your image into a multiple hyperlink called an image map.

Figure 3-1 displays NASA's Earth Observatory Web page, which contains both GIF and JPEG images.

HTML

Figure 3-1 NASA Earth Observatory Web page in browser

GIF images

GIF image

JPEG images

JPEG images

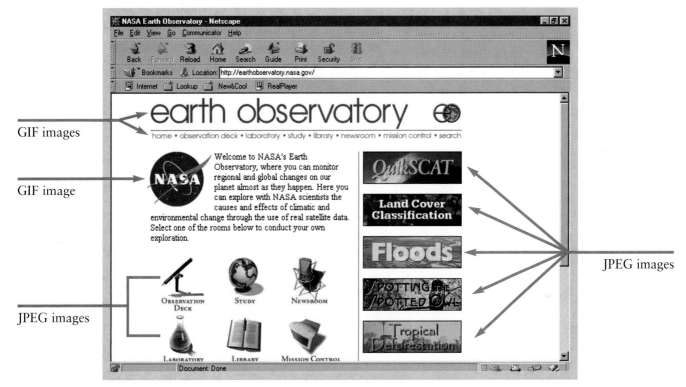

Skill Inserting Images

Concept

After you have saved an image in a manageable size and the appropriate format, use the Image tag and the Source attribute to insert it onto your Web page. These commands instruct the browser to locate and open the image. As long as you write your tags correctly, and save your images in the same folder as the Web page, you should have no trouble. Take advantage of the creative ways you can design pages with images. For example, you can group several small images together and create hyperlinks to construct a navigation bar for your site.

Do It!

Tom will insert an image onto a new page that he will create in Notepad.

1. Locate your Student Files folder, and open file Doit3-2 in Notepad.

2. Click File. Click Save As. Save the file as locations.

3. Place the insertion point after the </TITLE> tag. Press Enter.

4. Type: <IMG SRC="Unbound.jpg">. This image is located in your Student Files folder. Make sure you move it to the same folder as your Web pages.

5. Click File. Click Save. Your HTML document should look like **Figure 3-2**.

6. Click File. Click Save As. Save the file as locations.html.

7. Open the locations page in your browser. It should look like **Figure 3-3**.

More

An icon may display, instead of your image, if you have made a coding error. You should check several things. First, make sure the file name, Unbound.jpg, is written correctly. If any part of the file name is omitted, the browser will not be able to locate the image. Second, make sure the image and the Web page are in the same folder. They must be in the same folder or the browser will not locate the file and the image will not display.

The <IMG> tag does not require a closing tag. Even when you add formatting attributes, a closing tag is not necessary. Browsers will correctly interpret that the formatting options apply to the inline image.

Figure 3-2 Image added in HTML document

Image tag

Source attribute

Image file name

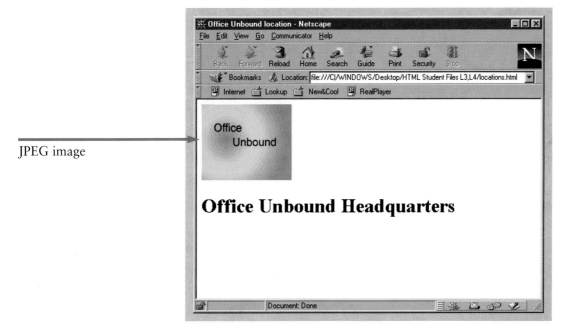

Figure 3-3 Image displayed in a browser

JPEG image

Practice

Add the **Prac3** image from your **Student Files** folder to the **Head** section of the **Index** page.

Hot Tip

When you are inserting an image below text, put the **<IMG>** tag inside **<P>** or **
** tags to place it on a line of its own.

Formatting Images

Concept

After an image has been added to a Web page, many formatting options are available. You can add a border, or align the image left, right or center. These simple formatting commands are constructed by adding attributes to the Image tag. Borders and image alignment can make your pages more attractive.

Do It!

Tom will add a border to the image he has inserted. He will also change the page alignment of the image.

1 Open the locations document in Notepad.

2 Place the insertion point between the closing quotation mark, ", and the closing angle bracket, >. Press the Space Bar.

3 Type: BORDER=5. Press the Space Bar. This attribute will place a border around the image.

4 Place the insertion point in front of the opening angle bracket, <. Type: <P ALIGN="center">.

5 Place the insertion point after the closing angle bracket, > of the Image tag. Type: </P>.

6 Click File. Click Save. Your file should look like **Figure 3-4**.

7 Click File. click Save As. Save the file as locations.html. Click [Yes] to overwrite the existing file.

8 If you open the locations page in a browser, it should look like **Figure 3-5**.

More

The method used to align the image in the steps above is the same method you would use to align text. Because the image is an inline graphic, it is treated the same as a piece of text, and can therefore be aligned, or have other similar functions performed on it.

The higher the value for the Border attribute, the thicker the image border will be. You can also align the image and text to the right, by typing ALIGN="right", and to the left, by typing ALIGN="left".

Figure 3-4 An image formatted in HTML

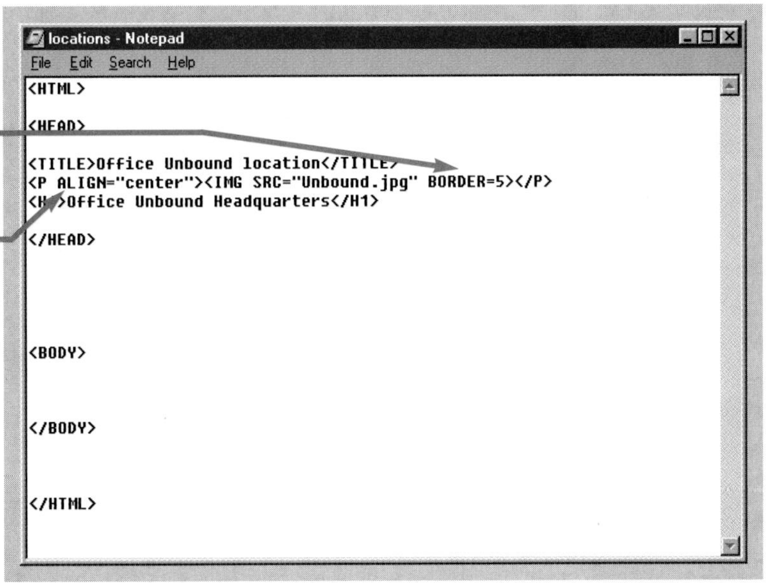

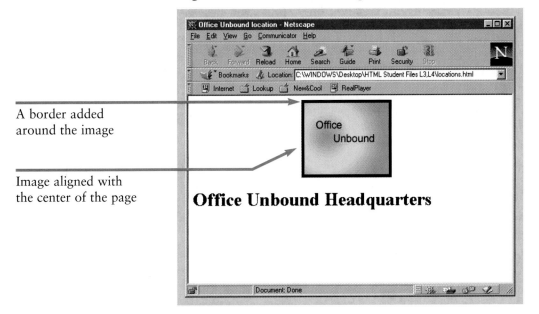

Adds a border
around the image

Aligns image

Figure 3-5 Formatted image in a browser

A border added
around the image

Image aligned with
the center of the page

Practice

Add a border to the image you inserted into the **Index** page earlier. Set the border thickness to **12**.

Hot Tip

You can set the Border attribute to **BORDER=0** to make sure that no border is inadvertently added to an image.

Skill Wrapping Text Around an Image

Concept

Text can be wrapped around an image using the Align attribute. Type ALIGN=left to align the image to the left while the text wraps to the right, or ALIGN=right to align the image to the right while the text wraps on the left. Text wrapping enables text to flow smoothly around logos, digital photographs and other images. Without the text wrapping capability many empty spaces would be left on your Web page.

Do It!

Rather than centering the image, Tom has decided he will reposition the image to the right, and wrap text around it instead.

1. Open the locations document in Notepad. Place the insertion point behind the closing angle bracket for the Paragraph tag, >, and the opening bracket for the Image tag, <. Press Delete until the entire Paragraph tag and attributes are deleted.

2. Place the insertion point behind the closing Paragraph tag. Press Delete until the closing Paragraph tag is deleted.

3. Place the insertion point between the end quotation mark from the Image Source value, and the Border attribute. Press the Space Bar.

4. Type: ALIGN=right.

5. Place the insertion point one line below the Header.

6. Type: <P>A place for people to come together and share an experience. A place for people to work as a team. A place to learn, share, and grow together. Office Unbound is indeed an office, unlike any you have ever known. Office Unbound is a unique experience, shared.</P>.

7. Type: <BR CLEAR=right>, to stop wrapping the text where there is no longer an image aligned to the right.

8. Click File. Click Save. Your document should look like **Figure 3-6**.

9. Click File. Click Save As. Save the file as locations.html. Click [Yes] to overwrite the existing file. If you open the locations page in your browser, it should look like **Figure 3-7**.

More

To wrap text between two images, first wrap the text around one image, then the other. Insert each image directly before the text that should flow around it. Each image will push the text to one side until there is a break or the text is complete.

To stop wrapping the text when there is no longer an image aligned on the left, type <BR CLEAR=left>. To stop a text wrap when you are wrapping text between two images, type <BR CLEAR=all>.

Figure 3-6 Wrapping text in an HTML document

All of the text that is to be wrapped

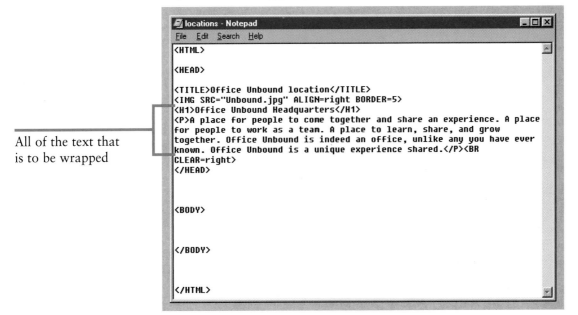

Figure 3-7 Wrapped text displayed in a browser

Text being wrapped around right-aligned image

Text wrap ends automatically where image ends

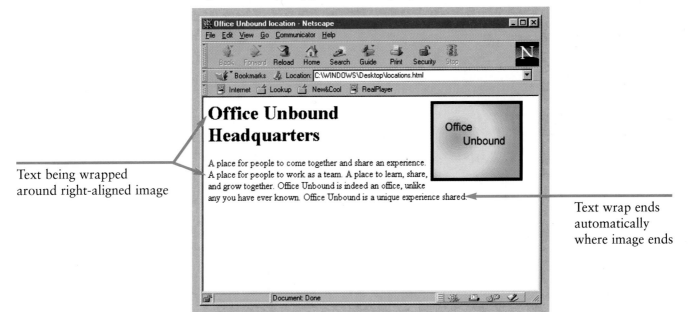

Practice

Keep the image you added earlier to the **Index** page aligned to the left. Wrap only the header around it.

Hot Tip

You should make sure not to get confused. You are aligning the image to the right or left, but the text will start wrapping on the opposite side. Also, make sure that you place the image before the text that will wrap around it.

 **Creating Image Maps**

Concept

Images can be ornamental *and* functional. You can make an image into a single hyperlink, or create multiple hyperlinks on one image. An image map contains any number of areas, also known as hotspots, that when clicked connect you to a different page or section. To create an image map you must specify the pixel coordinates of each hotspot.

Do It!

Tom is going to link to both the home page and the advantage page from the image on the locations page.

1 Open the locations document in Notepad.

2 Place the insertion point between the 5 value for the BORDER attribute, and the closing angle bracket, >. Press Space Bar.

3 Type: USEMAP="#Unbound"

4 Place the insertion point two lines below the closing Head tag.

5 Type: <MAP NAME="Unbound">. Press Enter.

6 Type: <AREA SHAPE="rect" COORDS="0,0,85,45" HREF="home.html">. Press Enter.

7 Type: <AREA SHAPE="rect" COORDS="50,50,148,121" HREF="advantage.html">. Press Enter.

8 Type: </MAP>.

9 Click File. Click Save. Your document should look like **Figure 3-8**.

10 Click File. Click Save As. Save the document as locations.html. Click [Yes] to overwrite the existing file.

11 Open the locations page in your browser. If you move the pointer over the image it will turn into a hand, 🖑. The upper-left corner of the image, including the word Office links to the home page, and the lower-right corner, including the word Unbound links to the advantage page. Your page should look like **Figure 3-9**.

More

For a rectangular area, coordinates are arranged so that the x, y coordinates for the upper left corner are first, and the coordinates for the lower right corner are second (x1, y1, x2, y2). You can make a circular region using the x, y coordinates for the center of the circle and the measurement of the radius, r. A polygonal area is created using coordinates for each point on the polygon (x1, y1, x2, y2, x3, y3)

Open your image in an image editor. When you move the pointer over the image the pixel coordinates should be displayed. If not use the Menu bar to open a window that will display the pixel coordinates of your image. This will give you the precise pixel coordinates to use for your hotspots.

Figure 3-8 Image Map specified in HTML

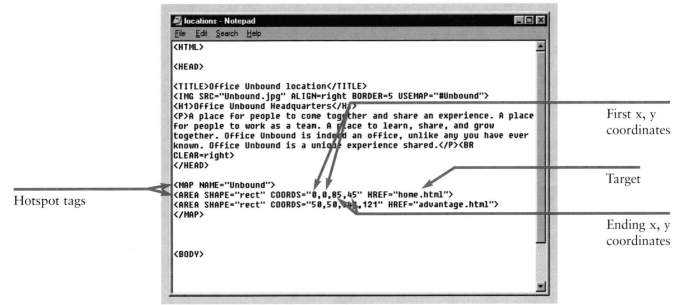

Hotspot tags

First x, y coordinates

Target

Ending x, y coordinates

Figure 3-9 Image map in a browser

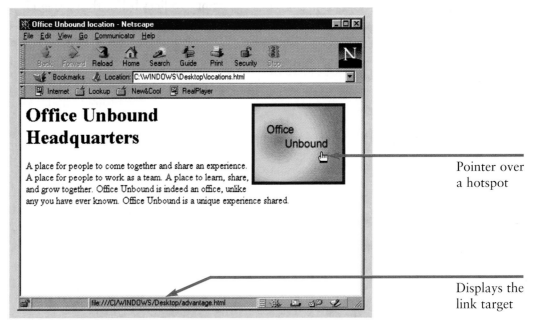

Pointer over a hotspot

Displays the link target

Practice

Create an image map using the image on the **Index** page. Make the hotspot whatever dimensions you would like. Link the image to the **Top Ten** page.

Hot Tip

If the areas overlap, the browser will usually use the link that was defined first. Don't put your clickable areas too close together or the user could click and go to the wrong page.

Adding Multimedia Files

Concept

The popularity of the Web has been fueled by the development of audio and video files and animation. The disadvantage of multimedia files is that they are often large, external files, which can take a long time to download. However, inline movies in AVI format and animated GIFs can be added to a Web page and played automatically. These files are collectively called multimedia files.

Do It!

Tom will add a small piece of animation to the home page.

1. Open the home document in Notepad.

2. Place the insertion point after the opening Head tag.

3. Press Enter.

4. Type: <IMG SRC="compass.gif">.

5. Click File. Click Save. Your document should look like **Figure 3-10**.

6. Click File, then click Save As. Save the document as home.html.

7. Click [Yes] to overwrite the existing file.

8. Open the home page in your browser. It should look like **Figure 3-11**.

More

The method described above is for adding an inline multimedia file. Internet Explorer allows you to add a background sound that plays automatically. The tag is <BGSOUND SRC="sound.ext"> (file name and extension). Netscape has a Live Audio plug-in that visitors can operate using Play, Stop and Volume control buttons. The <EMBED SRC="sound.ext"> tag instructs the browser to play the sound in the Web page itself. A plug-in is an enhancement added to a program to perform a specific function.

One way to deal with large audio and video files is to keep them external and create a link. The link can be an icon, picture or descriptive piece of text. Make the destination target the external multimedia file. Your page will load quickly and the visitor can decide whether or not to wait to access the file. For example, in Netscape, you can use the tag, <A HREF="sound.ext"> (the location and extension of the file) to allow visitors to choose whether or not to access large audio files.

Just like images, multimedia files and the Web page you want them to be displayed with must be kept in the same folder. The browser will not be able to locate the inline file, or link to the external file, if you neglect to do this.

Figure 3-10 Animation inserted in HTML

The animation is saved as a GIF file, and treated as an image

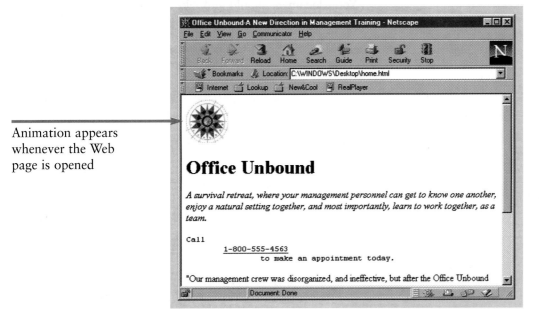

```
home - Notepad
File  Edit  Search  Help
<HTML>

<HEAD>
<IMG SRC="compass.gif">
<TITLE>Office Unbound-A New Direction in Management Training</title>
<H1>Office Unbound</H1>
</HEAD>

<BODY>
<I>A survival retreat, where your management personnel can get to know
one another, enjoy a natural setting together, and most importantly,
learn to work together, as a team.</I>

<PRE>Call
        <U>1-800-555-4563</U>
                 to make an appointment today.</Pre>

<P>"Our management crew was disorganized, and ineffective, but after
the Office Unbound experience they're functioning as one big team."</P>
<BR>Nancy Villones</BR>
<BR>CEO of Marthop Enterprises</BR>
<P><A HREF="advantage.html">Advantages of Coming to Office
Unbound</A></P>

</BODY>
```

Figure 3-11 Animation displayed in a browser

Animation appears whenever the Web page is opened

```
Office Unbound-A New Direction in Management Training - Netscape
File  Edit  View  Go  Communicator  Help

Back  Forward  Reload  Home  Search  Guide  Print  Security  Stop

Bookmarks    Location: C:\WINDOWS\Desktop\home.html

Internet   Lookup   New&Cool   RealPlayer
```

Office Unbound

A survival retreat, where your management personnel can get to know one another, enjoy a natural setting together, and most importantly, learn to work together, as a team.

```
Call
        1-800-555-4563
                 to make an appointment today.
```

"Our management crew was disorganized, and ineffective, but after the Office Unbound

`Document: Done`

HTML

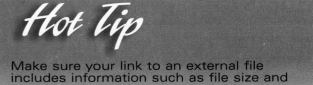

Practice

Create a link on the **Top Ten** page. The link should be, **"Can I help you?"(20.2kb)**. Link this to the file **Sound3.wav** in your **Student Files** folder. After the link write text that says, **This is Don Knobly's secretary Lisa Wessly**.

Hot Tip

Make sure your link to an external file includes information such as file size and format so users can decide whether or not to download it.

Skill Using Character Tags to Format Text

Concept

A particularly effective way to emphasize a section of text is to apply character tags to several characters or words. You have already learned several character tags: <BIG>, <B> (bold) and <I> (italic). Other character tags, such as the subscript and superscript tags, are useful for certain abbreviations and for mathematical and scientific formulas. The <CODE> tag can be used to create a mono-spaced font for URLs, computer code, and other text you want to offset from the main text. Internet Explorer even supports the <BLINK> tag with which you can emphasize a pertinent word, or a hyperlink.

Do It!

Tom will use character tags to format text on the home page.

1 Open the home document in Notepad.

2 Place the insertion point after the opening tag for the hyperlink at the bottom of the page.

3 Type: <EM><STRONG>. The <EM> tag stands for emphasizing and generally applies italics. The <STRONG> tag displays bold text.

4 Place the insertion point after Unbound.

5 Type: </STRONG></EM>.

6 Click File. Click Save. Your document should look like **Figure 3-12**.

7 Click File. Click Save As. Save the file as home.html. If you open the page in your browser it should look like **Figure 3-13**.

More

There are two types of character tags, logical and physical. Logical character tags specify how you want to use the text rather than how to display it. The browser decides how to display the text. Physical tags allow you to specify exactly what format changes you want the browser to display. For example, <STRONG> and <EM> are logical tags because while they tell browsers that you want to emphasize text, the browser decides how to emphasize it. The <B> and <I> tags are physical tags because they tell the browser to display bold and italics.

As you saw in the exercise, you can add character tags to hyperlinks. The default hyperlink color is blue, but you can change the color of links that have not been visited using LINK=. Use VLINK= to change the color of visited links and ALINK= to change hyperlink color when a visitor clicks it. After the equal sign, enter the hexadecimal code or one of the 16 predefined colors.

Figure 3-12 Character tags added to an HTML document

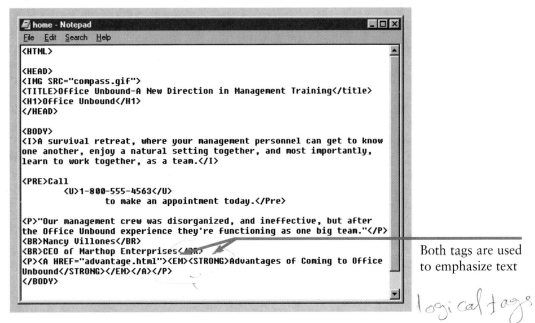

Both tags are used
to emphasize text

logical tags

Figure 3-13 Character tags applied in a browser

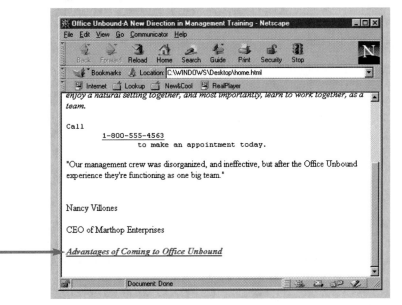

Hyperlink is
emphasized with
character tags

Practice

Use one of the character tags you learned on the previous page to format six list items on the **Top Ten** page.

Hot Tip

Character tags are so named because rather than affecting the entire document, or an object in the document, they can be used on individual characters.

Adding Special Characters to Text

Concept

You can create special characters such as accented and other foreign letters, dollar and cent signs, the ampersand (&), ellipsis, number (#) and at (@) symbols, using HTML code. The copyright, registered, and trademark symbols can also be inserted. These symbols are coded using the ampersand followed by the # sign and a number between 127 and 255.

Do It!

Tom needs to add the registered mark symbol to the name of the company in the Head section of the home page.

1. Open the home document in Notepad.

2. Place the insertion point between Unbound and the </H1> tag.

3. Type: ®. This is the code for the registered mark symbol.

4. Click File. Click Save.

5. Click File. Click Save As. Your document should look like **Figure 3-14**.

6. Save the document as home.html.

7. Click [Yes] to overwrite the existing file.

8. Open the home page in your browser. The page should look like **Figure 3-15**.

More

Typing &, followed by #, alerts the browser that what follows is a special character. Some other common special characters are the greater than and less than symbols and the percent (%)sign. Many special characters are foreign letters, which can prove useful in certain instances. For example, the occasion may arise where you need the Spanish "tilde" or the French "accent grave" to correctly spell a proper name. A math teacher may need Greek letters to write formulas for an online class or a "homework help" page. HTML special characters enable you to accomplish these tasks.

There is a list of special characters and their codes in the appendix at the end of this book.

Figure 3-14 Special character code in an HTML document

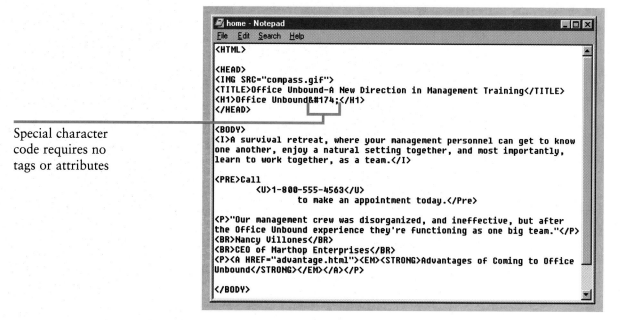

Special character
code requires no
tags or attributes

Figure 3-15 Special character in a browser

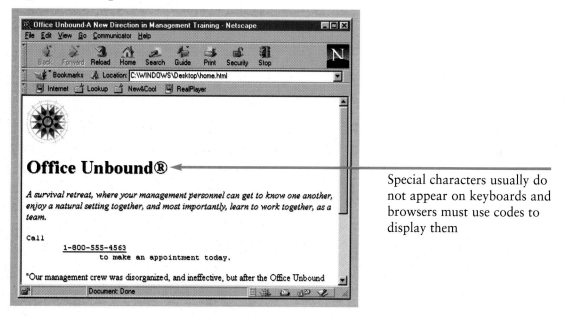

Special characters usually do
not appear on keyboards and
browsers must use codes to
display them

Practice

Place the code **©** and type: the date
in the last line before the closing Body tag
on the **Index** page.

Hot Tip

Some special characters have name codes
that make it easier to add them. Use the
appendix at the end of this book to view
the name codes.

HT 3.17

Skill Creating an E-mail Link

Concept

You can create links that allow a user to send electronic mail (e-mail) to a specified address. E-mail links to the Webmaster– generally the creator and/or manager of a site– are common. E-mail links can also be used to request information, contact key company personnel, or inquire about services. When the user clicks the link, their browser's e-mail program opens to a mail-composing window with the specified address already inserted.

Do It!

Tom will create a link that allows visitors to e-mail Office Unbound.

1. Open the home document in Notepad.

2. Place the insertion point after the the closing EM, Strong, and Paragraph tags at the bottom of the page.

3. Press Enter.

4. Type: <A HREF="mailto:info@officeunbound.domain.com">E-mail us for more information</A>.

5. Press Enter.

6. Click File. Click Save. Your document should look like **Figure 3-16**.

7. Click File. Click Save As.

8. Save the document as home.html.

9. Click [Yes] to overwrite the existing file.

10. Open the home page in your browser.

11. Click the E-mail us for more information link. If you are using a Netscape browser, your screen will look like **Figure 3-17**.

More

You can also link to a newsgroup. To create a link to a newsgroup, type: <A HREF="news:newsgroup.group">. This link will allow visitors to link to the specified newsgroup the same way they can link to an e-mail address or link to another Web page document.

Often a good way to indicate that a link goes to an e-mail address is to make the e-mail address the actual link. For example, type: <A HREF="mailto:name@server.net">name@server.net</A>. This will create a link that is exactly the same as the e-mail address.

Figure 3-16 Link to e-mail in an HTML document

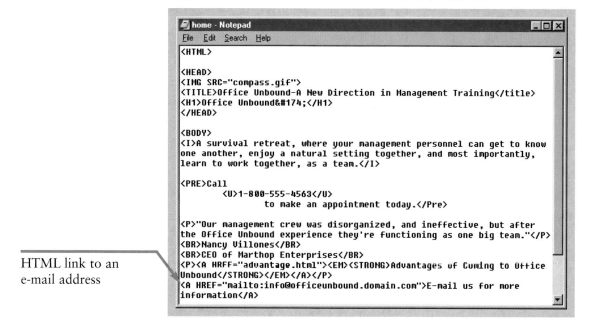

HTML link to an
e-mail address

Figure 3-17 An e-mail link to a mail program

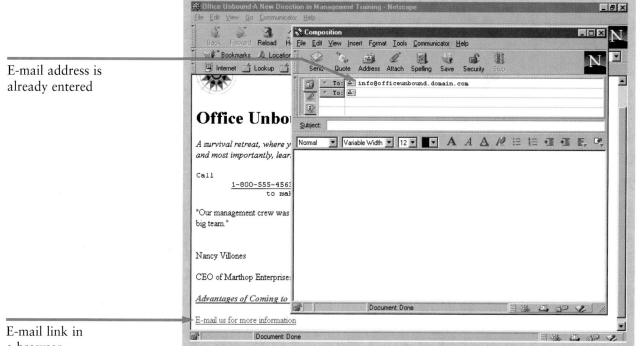

E-mail address is
already entered

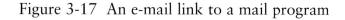

E-mail link in
a browser

Practice

Create a link at the bottom of the **Index** page that says, **E-mail Don Knobly**. The e-mail address is **DKnobly@personalaccount.domain.com**.

Hot Tip

E-mail links are not standard HTML. Although no browser claims to support them, they work in both Internet Explorer and Netscape Navigator.

Skill

Using Pathnames

Concept

Pathnames are used to specify the location of a file. They identify the path that will be taken to find the file. The path to some files can be quite complex, for instance, in a subfolder of a subfolder of a folder.

To create links or insert images or multimedia files, you will need to know their pathnames. If you do not formulate the pathname correctly, the browser will be unable to locate the image or page. You will wind up with images that do not display and hyperlinks that do not function.

There are two types of pathnames, relative and absolute. Relative pathnames do not specify the exact location (i.e. what folders a file is in). Instead, they describe where a file is in relation to the current location (where the file is from here). In order for a relative pathname to work, the file being referenced must be in the same folder as the present location. The relative pathname for a file in the same folder will simply be the file name and extension ("sound.wav"). For a file that is in a subfolder inside the current folder, the pathname will be the subfolder name followed by a forward slash and then the file name and extension (sounds/sound.wav).

If you use an absolute pathname, the files do not have to be in the same folder. An absolute pathname specifies the exact location, or address, of a file. Absolute pathnames have no relationship to the current location. The advantage to using absolute pathnames is that they do not change as long as you do not move a file (e.g. a permanent address). Absolute pathnames must be used for newsgroups, e-mail links and any file that does not use HTTP (Hypertext Transfer Protocol). The disadvantage is that they can be long and tedious to type. You should use relative pathnames whenever possible because they are short– thus there is less chance of making an error. As long as the relative position of each file stays the same, your images will be located and your links will work.

To locate a link, image, or other file that you would like to use in an HTML document with relative pathnames, you must first ensure that the HTML document and the file you want to use are located in the same folder. Relative pathnames are generally used for hyperlinks and linking to other documents on your Web pages.

To find the absolute pathname of a file, use Windows Explorer. Use the View menu to open the Toolbar submenu. Then activate the Address bar. A portion of the absolute pathname of any file you want to use will display in the Address bar at the top of the screen, as shown in **Figure 3-18**. Highlight the partial absolute pathname, and copy it into your HTML document. Be sure to enter the filename at the end of the partial absolute pathname to make it a complete pathname.

Figure 3-18 The absolute pathname to locate Internet Explorer

The path taken to locate these files

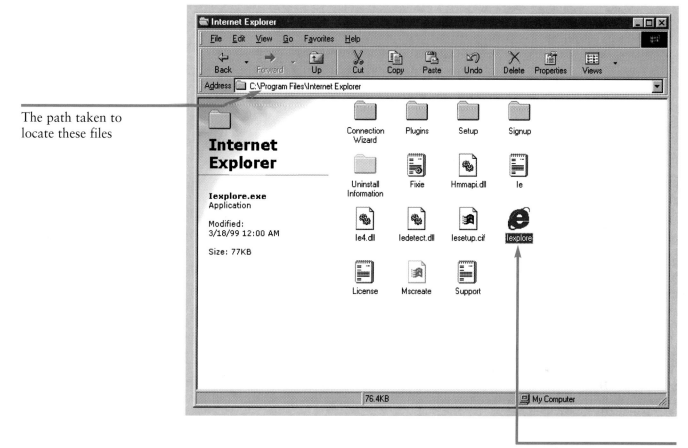

File located within the Internet Explorer folder

Pathnames actually become URLs when the pages are published. For example, relative pathnames will be the URLs the browser will use to locate and open your Web pages and images.

Shortcuts

Character Tag	Function	Logical/Physical
<B>	Makes text bold	physical
<BIG>	Displays text in a big font	physical
<CITE>	A short citation or quotation	logical
<CODE>	Indicates text should be displayed in a mono-spaced font	logical
<EM>	Emphasizes text, usually by italicizing it	logical
<I>	Italicizes text	physical
<KBD>	Specifies keyboard text	logical
<SMALL>	Displays text in a small font	physical
<STRONG>	Emphasizes text, usually bolding it	logical
<SUB>	Displays text as subscript	physical
<SUP>	Displays text as superscript	physical
<TT>	Displays font with same width for each character	physical
<VAR>	Displays a variable, often italicized or underlined	logical

Identify Key Features

Name the items indicated by callouts in **Figure 3-19**

Figure 3-19 Advanced features in an HTML document

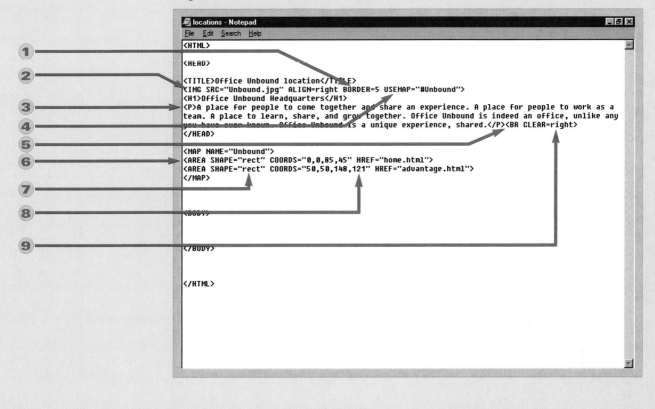

Select The Best Answer

10. Does not require a closing tag

11. Coordinates for a circle are listed this way

12. Use this attribute to center an image

13. A type of multimedia file

14. One of the most common file types for saving images

15. Formats text based on how text is used

16. Formats characters exactly as you want them to look

17. Formats characters

18. Adds characters you can't add from a keyboard

a. ALIGN

b. JPEG

c. Logical tags

d. Image tag

e. Physical tags

f. Character tags

g. Sound

h. x, y, r

i. Special characters

Complete the Statement

19. An image that is displayed with a Web page without being downloaded separately is called:

    a. A multimedia file

    b. An inline image

    c. An image map

    d. An animation

20. When you insert an image, this attribute is the one that tells the browser where to find the image:

    a. IMG

    b. BORDER

    c. USEMAP

    d. SRC

21. To completely erase the border around an image, the value of the BORDER attribute should be:

    a. 0

    b. 1

    c. 3

    d. NONE

22. To wrap text around the right side of an image, the Image attribute and value should be:

    a. ALIGN=right

    b. ALIGN=left

    c. ALIGN=center

    d. ALIGN=justify

23. If the coordinates for a hotspot are 12, 12, 43, 55, 123, 77, the shape of the hotspot is:

    a. A circle

    b. A rectangle

    c. A polygon

    d. An ellipse

24. An image which you want to insert has a very large file size. You should:

    a. Only send it by request to people who e-mail you

    b. Add it directly to the Web page

    c. Create a link on the page that connects directly to the file

    d. Cut it into multiple pieces and only display it a piece at a time

25. Type this first so that browsers can decipher the special character code which follows:

    a. @

    b. &

    c. #

    d. %

Interactivity

Test Your Skills

1. Insert and format an image:

    a. Open the sunglass document in Notepad.

    b. Insert the image test3.jpg into the body of the document.

    c. Set the border for the image at 3.

    d. Wrap the text that appears contained in a <BIG> tag around the right side of the image.

    e. Save the sunglass document.

2. Create an image map:

    a. Open the sunglass document in Notepad.

    b. Create a circular hotspot on the image. The USEMAP name is logo. Link the hotspot to the prices page.

    c. The coordinates are 85, 68, 40. This will create the circular hotspot.

    d. Save the sunglass document. Save it again as sunglass.html. Move the pointer over the image to find the hotspot. Test it to make sure it works.

3. Use character tags and special characters:

    a. Open the sunglass document in Notepad.

    b. Add a <VAR> character tag to all of the unordered list items on the sunglass page.

    c. Add two special characters to the sunglass page. First add a registered mark symbol after the name of the company, Sunglass City. Then add a copyright symbol and the date at the bottom of the page. Use the reference guide in the appendix to find the proper codes.

    d. Save the sunglass document.

4. Create an e-mail link:

    a. Open the sunglass page in Notepad.

    b. At the bottom of the sunglass page, create a link to the e-mail address Greg@sunglasscity.domain/ceo.com. The link should be the same as the e-mail address.

    c. Save the sunglass document.

HTML

Interactivity (continued)

Problem Solving

1. Excellent job! The executives at The Fixit Company are happy with your work. Now, it is time to enhance the Web site using some of the more advanced features of HTML. Open the Fixit document. First you must add an image to the Web site. This should be a logo you design yourself, but if you have access to an appropriate photo, you may use that instead. Make sure that you save the logo as a GIF or JPEG. Place the image on the top-left side of the page. Also create an image map. Use a shape and coordinates that conform to an area on your image, and link the area to the Options page. If you have access to an appropriate video, animation, or sound file, insert it into the Fixit page. However, the executives at The Fixit Company do not want the page to take a long time to download, so keep that in mind. Finally, save the document as Fixit.

2. Open the Options page. First, use character tags to format the payment options list. Apply the <STRONG> tag to emphasize the list items. Next, use the special character code, &#36, to add the dollar sign to the appropriate table items. Format the final paragraph, which contains the phone number, using the <SMALL> tags. Finally, create an e-mail link at the bottom of the page. Make the e-mail address: info@fixit.domain.com, the link. Add a copyright symbol and the date below the e-mail link. Use the reference guide in the appendix to find the correct code. Save the document as Options.

3. Open the Personal document you worked on earlier. It is time to use advanced HTML features to format your Web site. Take out your plans, outline and list of favorite elements. First, decide what images to use. You may publish images that you create yourself, but if you use other people's work, you must get copyright permission. Format the image to enhance the visual appeal of your site. Design your page layout, determining where the image would look best and if you should wrap text around it. Create as many pages as you want. Then, design your site structure, and link the pages together. When you are finished, save your document as Personal. If you added any objects or made changes to the Index page, save them too.

4. Several more elements should be added to the Index and Personal pages. At the bottom of one of these pages, add an e-mail link. The target destination should be your own e-mail address. Make the label anything you want. It can be a piece of text, your e-mail address, an image, or simply your name. Use character tags to format some text on each of these two pages. You may want to emphasize something, apply italics, or use a subscript or superscript. If necessary, use special character codes to apply dollar or cent signs, or insert a trademark, copyright or registered symbol. When all of your formatting changes are complete, save the two documents as Index and Personal.

Skills

L E S S O N

4

CREATING FORMS AND PUBLISHING WEB PAGES

Have you ever purchased a product on the Internet? Participated in a survey? Entered a contest or registered for a site? All of these experiences are interactive. Communication is a two-sided affair. So far in this book, we have concentrated on effective and engaging ways to communicate your ideas to others. This lesson will teach you how your Web site visitors can communicate with you. Forms help to make the Web a dynamic interactive experience.

Forms enable visitors to submit information back to a Web site. They contain data entry fields called input fields or controls. There are two parts to a form: the form structure, consisting of the data entry fields, labels and buttons; and the processing script, or application, which converts the submitted information into a usable format.

In this lesson you will learn how to create the controls- text entry boxes, radio buttons, check boxes, pull-down menus, and scroll boxes– that visitors will use to answer questions or provide information. You will learn which input fields are most efficient for various question types and how to formulate the HTML commands to construct them. Creating the controls is no more difficult than the other HTML coding you have learned thus far.

Processing forms is much more complicated and is beyond the scope of this book. However, you will become familiar with the concepts and terminology, and will learn a simple method for submitting unprocessed forms to your own e-mail address.

Next, you will learn how to register keywords with a search engine, so that visitors can find your page. Finally, you will be given some helpful hints on Web site publishing.

Case Study:
Tom Randes wants to create an order form for Office Unbound. He will create the necessary input fields to produce a useful and effective form. He will also tell search engines what the site is about so that prospective customers can find it.

Skill **Using Forms**

Concept

You can use forms on your Web site to take orders for goods and services, conduct surveys, get visitor feedback, register visitors, and many other activities. Visitors can respond to your requests for information by easily filling in text boxes, clicking radio buttons, using pull-down menus, or scrolling lists. Forms make information gathering simple and highly efficient.

If you have surfed the Web to any extent, you are probably familiar with the various controls we will create in this lesson. Text entry boxes typically contain one line of text and are used in situations where the information will be unique to each individual user, such as name, user ID or password. Radio buttons and check boxes limit the type of information a visitor can enter. Several options are presented from which the user must choose. Pull-down menus and scroll boxes present lists of possible answers. They are generally used in situations where there are many choices.

The two push buttons common to all forms are the Submit and Reset buttons. The Submit button sends the information to the server. The Reset button enables the user to start over with a new form set to the default values you have designated. You may be familiar with other push buttons such as the Log On and Log Off buttons present on some Web sites.

Processing forms generally requires a simple application called a CGI (Common Gateway Interface) script to work. This program communicates with the server to take the information submitted by visitors and send it back to the Web site in a readable format. Your ISP (Internet Service Provider) may or may not allow you to run a CGI script for security reasons. However, there are form-hosting services that will process your forms and e-mail the collated results back to you, at no charge, if you allow them to run a banner ad on your form page. CGI scripts are generally written in a programming language called PERL. However if you don't know PERL, there are many ready-to-use CGI scripts available on the Web.

In this lesson we will show you how to format the HTML instructions that will submit each form individually to your e-mail address. You will receive them in an unprocessed format. Each submission will consist of name-value pairs corresponding to the controls you have created for the form. For example, name=smith &email=smith @aol.com &payment=Visa. This method will suffice for personal Web sites where your respondents will be few. You will be able to interpret and collate the information yourself, but business sites will require a CGI script on a server, or a form-hosting service.

Figure 4-1 displays a guest book form from the NASA Web site that includes text entry fields and push buttons.

Figure 4-2 displays the HTML for the guest book page form shown in **Figure 4.1**. It includes some of the tags you will be learning in this lesson, and shows you how your HTML document may look when you create a form.

Figure 4-1 A guestbook form in a browser

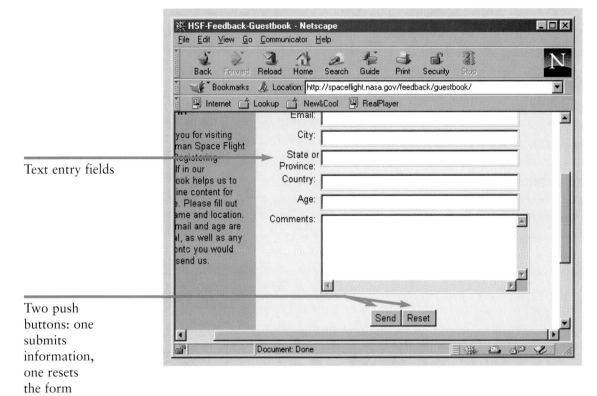

Text entry fields

Two push
buttons: one
submits
information,
one resets
the form

HTML

Figure 4-2 HTML source of guestbook

Text entry field
in HTML

Two push buttons
in HTML

```
Source of: http://spaceflight.nasa.gov/feedback/guestbook/ - Netscape

    <TR>
     <td ALIGN="right" width="189" valign="top">
      <font face="arial, helvetica"" size="-1">Age: </font>
     </td>
     <td width="399" align="left" valign="top">
      <INPUT TYPE="text" NAME="age" SIZE=35 MAXLENGTH=35>
     </td>
    </TR>

    <TR>
     <td ALIGN="right" width="189" valign="top">
      <font face="arial, helvetica"" size="-1">Comments: </font>
     </td>
     <td width="399" align="left" valign="top">
      <TEXTAREA NAME="comments" ROWS=5 COLS=35></TEXTAREA>
     </td>
    </TR>

        <TR><TD> </TD></TR>
        <TR>
          <TD ALIGN=CENTER COLSPAN=2>
          <INPUT TYPE="submit" VALUE="Send"><INPUT TYPE="reset"
          </TD>
        </TR>
     </TABLE>
       <BR>
```

 # Adding Text Entry Fields

Concept

Text entry fields are text boxes that allow users to enter information. You can specify the size and type of a text entry field when you are creating it. Text entry fields are typically used to collect names, addresses, credit card numbers and other information that is unique to the visitor.

Do It!

Tom will create a form and add text entry fields to collect information for Office Unbound.

1. Open the document Doit4-4 in Notepad.

2. Click File. Click Save As. Save the document as form, in the same location as the rest of your pages.

3. Place the insertion point two lines below the opening Body tag.

4. Type: <FORM>. Press Enter.

5. Type: <P>Name: <INPUT TYPE="TEXT" SIZE=27 NAME="name"></P>. Press Enter.

6. Type: <P>Address: <INPUT TYPE="TEXT" SIZE=25 NAME="address"></P>. Press Enter.

7. Type: <P>City: <INPUT TYPE="TEXT" SIZE=28 NAME="city">. Press Enter.

8. Type: State: <INPUT TYPE="TEXT" SIZE=2 NAME="state">. Press Enter.

9. Type: Zip Code: <INPUT TYPE="TEXT" SIZE=5 NAME="zip"></P>. Press Enter.

10. Type: </FORM>.

11. Click File. Click Save. The document should look like **Figure 4-3**.

12. Click File, click Save As. Save the page as form.html. If you open the page in your browser, it should look like **Figure 4-4**.

More

The value for text box size is measured in characters. Characters include letters and spaces. The size attribute limits the number of characters that may be entered into the field. For example, setting the State field to 2 limits users to entering the state abbreviation. The default size for a text box is twenty characters.

If you want to create a large text box, use the tag <TEXTAREA>. Add the attributes NAME, ROWS=the number of rows in the text box, COLS=the number of columns, and WRAP to keep the text within the margins.

Figure 4-3 A form added to an HTML document

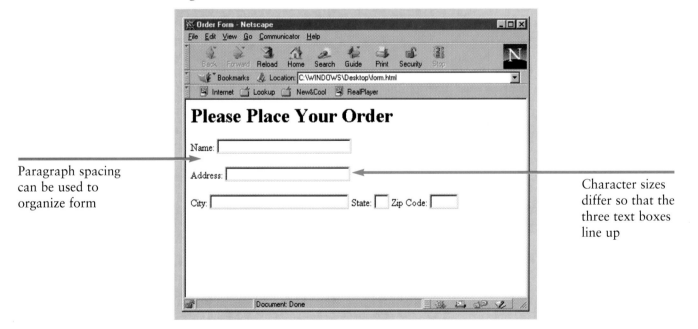

Specifies that input field is a text box

Size measured in characters

Figure 4-4 Text boxes in a browser

Paragraph spacing can be used to organize form

Character sizes differ so that the three text boxes line up

Practice

Begin by creating a new document. Start by writing the basic HTML structure, then create a text entry field that asks for the users **name**, **phone number**, **address**, **city**, **state**, and **annual income**. Save the document as **account**.

Hot Tip

To create a password box, enter **PASSWORD** as the **INPUT TYPE**. All other attributes can be the same. When the visitor fills in the field, bullets or asterisks will hide the letters, depending on which browser you are using.

Inserting Check Boxes and Radio Buttons

Concept

Check boxes and radio buttons are similar in that they limit visitors to one or more options. Radio buttons offer a group of options from which only one can be chosen. Check boxes are often used to answer yes or no questions, but can also be created in situations where you want to allow multiple selections. A set of check boxes can be presented from which the user checks all answers that apply. Both input fields facilitate data entry by allowing visitors to answer questions with a few clicks of the mouse.

Do It!

Tom wants to add a check box and some radio buttons to the form page.

1 Open the form document in Notepad.

2 Place the insertion point after the final closing Paragraph tag. Press Enter twice.

3 Type: <P>Please choose a payment method:</P>. Press Enter.

4 Type: <INPUT TYPE="RADIO" NAME="payment" VALUE="credit">Credit. Press Enter. Type: <INPUT TYPE="RADIO" NAME="payment" VALUE="debit">Debit. Press Enter. Type: <INPUT TYPE="RADIO" NAME="payment" VALUE="check">Check. Press Enter twice.

5 Type: <P>You may check more than one:</P>. Press Enter. Type: <P>Why would you like to attend Office Unbound?</P>. Press Enter.

6 Type: <INPUT TYPE="CHECKBOX" NAME="attend" VALUE="fun">Fun. Press Enter. Type: <INPUT TYPE="CHECKBOX" NAME="attend" VALUE="learn">Learn survival techniques. Press Enter. Type: <INPUT TYPE="CHECKBOX" NAME="attend" VALUE="meet">Meet new people. Press Enter. Type: <INPUT TYPE="CHECKBOX" NAME="attend" VALUE="know">Know my coworkers better. Press Enter twice.

7 Click File. Click Save. Your document should look like **Figure 4-5**.

8 Click File. Click Save As. Save the file as form.html. Click [Yes] to overwrite the existing file. If you open your page in your browser, it should look like **Figure 4-6**.

More

Keyboard shortcuts can be created for radio buttons and check boxes. Inside the Input Type tag, add the attribute ACCESSKEY=a, where a represents any letter of the alphabet. Add (Alt-A) or (ALT+A) next to the text box label to let visitors know that keyboard shortcuts are available. You can create a keyboard shortcut for each check box in a set.

Figure 4-5 Radio buttons and check boxes in an HTML document

```
form - Notepad
File  Edit  Search  Help

<BODY>

<FORM>
<P>Name: <INPUT TYPE="TEXT" SIZE=27 NAME="name">
<P>Address: <INPUT TYPE="TEXT" SIZE=25 NAME="address">
<P>City: <INPUT TYPE="TEXT" SIZE=28 NAME="city">
State: <INPUT TYPE="TEXT" SIZE=2 NAME="state">
Zip Code: <INPUT TYPE="TEXT" SIZE=5 NAME></P>

<P>Please choose a payment method:</P>
<INPUT TYPE="RADIO" NAME="payment" VALUE="credit">Credit
<INPUT TYPE="RADIO" NAME="payment" VALUE="debit">Debit
<INPUT TYPE="RADIO" NAME="payment" VALUE="check">Check

<P>You may check more than one:</P>
<P>Why would you like to attend Office Unbound?</P>
<INPUT TYPE="CHECKBOX" NAME="attend" VALUE="Fun">Fun
<INPUT TYPE="CHECKBOX" NAME="attend" VALUE="learn">Learn survival
techniques
<INPUT TYPE="CHECKBOX" NAME="attend" VALUE="meet">Meet new people
<INPUT TYPE="CHECKBOX" NAME="attend" VALUE="know">Know my coworkers
better

</FORM>
```

Tag used to create radio buttons

Tag used to create check boxes

HTML

Figure 4-6 Radio buttons and check boxes in a browser

Order Form - Netscape
File Edit View Go Communicator Help

Back Forward Reload Home Search Guide Print Security Stop

Bookmarks Location: C:\WINDOWS\Desktop\form.html

Internet Lookup New&Cool RealPlayer

Name:
Address: [   ]
City: [   ] State: [ ] Zip Code: [   ]

Please choose a payment method:

C Credit C Debit C Check

You may check more than one:

Why would you like to attend Office Unbound?

□ Fun □ Learn survival techniques □ Meet new people □ Know my coworkers better

Document: Done

A group of radio buttons. You may only select one

A group of check boxes. You may select more than one

Practice

Create a group of radio buttons on the **account** page. The text is, **How did you hear about us?** The buttons should read **Newspaper**, **The Web**, and **Word of mouth**. Then add one check box, with the text, **Have we served you before?**.

Hot Tip

Check boxes and radio buttons are linked in a group by the **NAME** attribute. It identifies them as members of a particular set. This allows multiple sets of boxes or buttons to occupy one form without confusing data analysis.

HT 4.7

Creating Pull-Down Menus and Scroll Boxes

Concept

Pull-down menus save space on your form when there are many choices. A set of ten check boxes or radio buttons would occupy considerable space. A pull-down menu will only display its list of options when the user clicks an arrow to open the menu. Scroll boxes display more than one item at a time and the user scrolls through to uncover the remaining options. Both input fields make it easy for visitors to answer questions or furnish search criteria.

Do It!

Tom will add a pull-down menu and a scroll box to the form page.

1 Open the form document in Notepad.

2 Place the insertion point after the word better. Press Enter twice.

3 Type: <P>How long will you be staying?</P>. Press Enter. Type: <SELECT NAME="staying">. Press Enter. Type: <OPTION SELECTED VALUE="week-end">Weekend. Press Enter. Type: <OPTION VALUE="3">3 Days. Press Enter. Type: <OPTION VALUE="5">5 Days. Press Enter. Type: <OPTION VALUE="7">1 Week. Press Enter. Type: </SELECT>.

4 Press Enter twice.

5 Type: <P>You may select more than one:</P>. Press Enter. Type: <P>During which month(s) would you like to visit?</P>. Press Enter.

6 Type: <SELECT NAME="month" SIZE=3>. Press Enter. Type: <OPTION SELECTED VALUE="april">April. Press Enter. Type: <OPTION VALUE="may">May. Press Enter. Type: <OPTION VALUE="june">June. Press Enter. <OPTION VALUE="july">JULY. Press Enter. <OPTION VALUE="august">August. Press Enter. Type: <OPTION VALUE="september">September. Press Enter. Type: <OPTION VALUE="october">October. Press Enter. Type: </SELECT>.

7 Click File. Click Save. Your document should look like **Figure 4-7**.

8 Click File. Click Save As, save the file as form.html. Click [Yes] to overwrite the existing file. If you open the form page in your browser, it should look like **Figure 4-8**.

More

The attributes added to the Select tag make it a scroll box or pull-down menu. If you specify a size, as in the skill above, that size specifies the number of options displayed, and the options are listed in a scroll box. If no size is given, then the options are displayed in a pull-down menu. You may also add the Multiple attribute. This attribute allows the user to select multiple options, and is displayed as a scroll box.

The value attached to each selection will be used later when the form is submitted. These values will be used to collect information, as you will see later in this lesson.

Figure 4-7   A pull-down menu and scroll box in an HTML document

Option tag indicates the options to be listed in the pull-down menu

Size indicates how many options are displayed

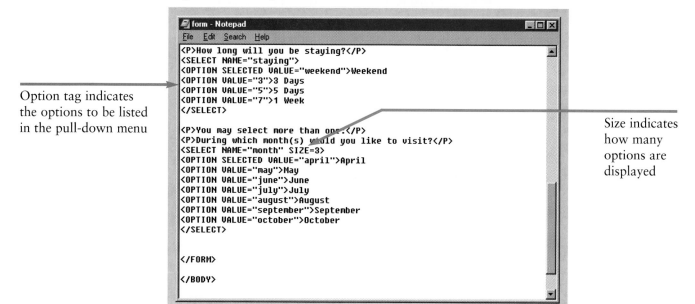

Figure 4-8   Pull-down menu and scroll box in a browser

Click arrow, then click option to make a selection

Three options displayed in scroll box

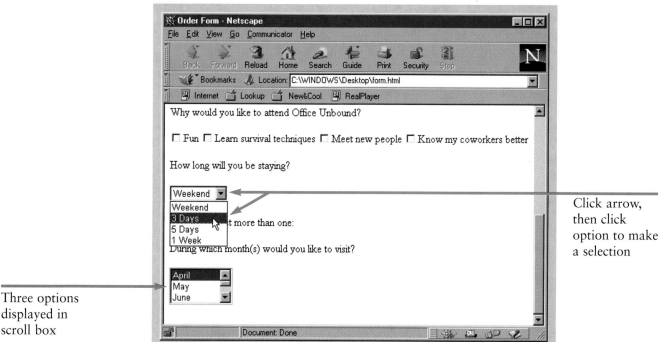

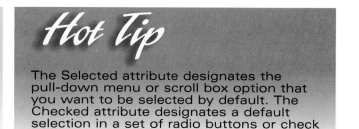

Practice

Create a pull-down menu. The text should read: **How many times have you been to an accountant?**. The options are, **0, 1-3, 4-8, 9-12, 13 or more**. You can select the default option. The menu will be on the **account** page.

Hot Tip

The Selected attribute designates the pull-down menu or scroll box option that you want to be selected by default. The Checked attribute designates a default selection in a set of radio buttons or check boxes.

Adding Push Buttons to a Form

Concept

Push buttons are used to perform preset functions on a form. The most common push buttons are the Submit and Reset buttons. If you want the information delivered, you must create a Submit button. Reset buttons allow the user to start the form over from scratch. The Submit and Reset buttons usually appear at the bottom of the form, but they can be placed anywhere that is convenient.

Do It!

Tom will add two push buttons to the form page.

1 Open the form document in Notepad.

2 Place the insertion point after the closing </SELECT> tag. Press Enter twice.

3 Type: <P><INPUT TYPE="SUBMIT" VALUE="Send Order">.

4 Press Enter.

5 Type: <INPUT TYPE="RESET" VALUE="Reset Form"></P>.

6 Click File. Click Save. Your document should look like **Figure 4-9**.

7 Click File. Click Save As.

8 Save the file as form.html.

9 Click [Yes] to overwrite the existing file.

10 Open the form page in your browser. It should look like **Figure 4-10**.

More

If you want a Submit or Reset button with an image, you will have to use the Button tag. For example, <BUTTON TYPE="submit" NAME="submit" VALUE="submit"<IMG SRC="compass.gif">Send Order</BUTTON>. Using the Button tags (as opposed to the Input Type tags), the value attribute does not designate the text that will appear on the button. The button text is entered before the closing button tag. The button tag is a new HTML 4 feature. Unfortunately, only Internet Explorer 4 for Windows supports it even though it is standard HTML 4.

If you do not enter a Value attribute for the Input Type tag, the default Submit message is Submit Query. The default Reset message is Reset.

Figure 4-9 Two push buttons in an HTML document

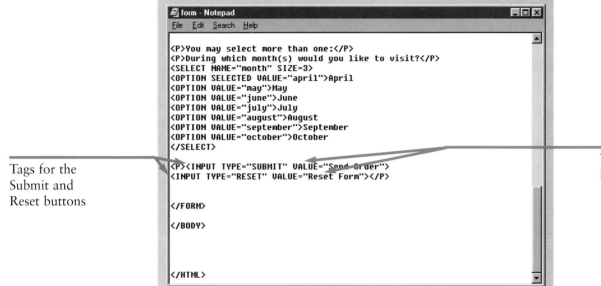

Tags for the
Submit and
Reset buttons

Value is the
button label

HTML

Figure 4-10 Push buttons displayed in a browser

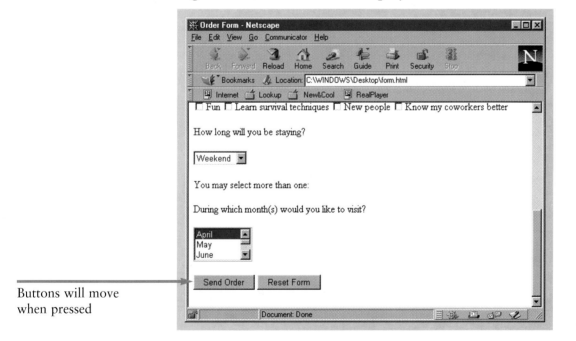

Buttons will move
when pressed

Practice

Add a submit and reset button to the bottom of the **account** page. The text on both buttons should simply be **Submit** and **Reset**.

Hot Tip

You can also change the font, font size and background color of a button with the Button tag. Use the Style attribute to designate the changes. For example, **STYLE= "font: 24 pt Arial Black; background:cyan"**.

Skill

Sending Information from a Form

Concept

As we said earlier, processing forms is a complex procedure beyond the scope of this book. This exercise describes a method for sending unprocessed forms, one-at-a-time, directly to an e-mail address. It will familiarize you with the HTML tags and attributes for submitting forms. Generally, the Form tag will include the URL of the CGI script, not an e-mail address. The Submit button will send the data to the CGI script on the server, to process your forms. The CGI script will take the name-value pairs (visitor_name=smith) from all the forms, parse and collate the data, and send a report back to your Web site.

Do It!

Tom will have the information collected from the form page sent to an e-mail address he specifies.

1. Open the form document in Notepad.

2. Place the insertion point inside the opening Form tag, before the second angle bracket, >.

3. Press the Space Bar.

4. Type: METHOD="POST"
   ACTION="mailto:orders@officeunbound.domain.com".

5. Click File. Click Save. Your document should look like **Figure 4-11**.

6. Click File. Click Save As.

7. Save the document as form.html.

8. Click [Yes] to overwrite the existing file.

9. **Figure 4-12** displays what the information collected from a form will look like when it is e-mailed.

More

There are two methods for sending information to the CGI script on the server: POST and GET. The POST method sends a file with the name-value pairs, the content type, and content length to the server where the CGI script analyzes the data. The GET method adds the name-value pairs to the end of the URL and passes the information on through another set of variables that must be broken down by the CGI script before they can be analyzed. In laymen's terms, the results of the two methods differ in that the GET method may result in data being abridged. For this reason, most people recommend the POST method.

As we said earlier, there are many ready-to-use CGI scripts to be found on the Web. You will simply have to download one, open it up, and change the pathnames and variables to suit your needs. Form hosting services will provide you with a form template to revise and edit as necessary.

Figure 4-11 Specifying how information is to be collected

Specifies where the information goes

Figure 4-12 Information from a form sent via e-mail

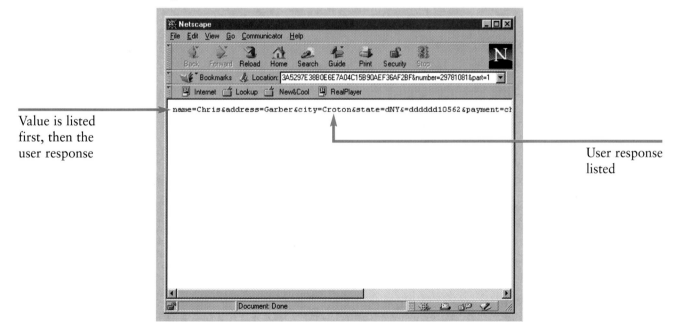

Value is listed first, then the user response

User response listed

Practice

Make sure that the information from the **account** page is sent to the e-mail address, **DKnobly@personalaccount.domain.com**.

Hot Tip

Most servers require that all CGI scripts be located in a cgi-bin directory.

Directing Visitors to a Web Site

Concept

As the Web expands, it becomes increasingly unlikely that Web surfers will accidentally happen upon your page. Most people use search engines to locate pages dealing with specific subjects. Users enter keywords to "tell" the search engine what they are looking for. You can use the META tag to designate keywords and describe your Web site for search engines.

Do It!

Tom will use the Meta tag so users searching for pages with similar topics will find the Office Unbound Web site.

1 Open the home document in Notepad.

2 Place the insertion point after the <HEAD> tag.

3 Press Enter.

4 Type: <META NAME="keywords" CONTENT="Office Unbound, management training, retreats, vacations, teamwork, survival techniques">.

5 Press Enter.

6 Type: <META NAME="descriptions" CONTENT="a new experience in management training, for learning teamwork">.

7 Press Enter.

8 Type: <META NAME="author" CONTENT="Tom Randes">.

9 Click File. Click Save. Your document should look like **Figure 4-13**.

More

You should carefully choose the words you use to describe your Web site. For example, the word management is too broad. More specific terms should weed out people who are not interested in management training retreats.

Many search engines provide tips on how to use the Meta tag effectively. If you have a favorite search engine, visit their Web site and read their tips to ensure that your Web page will be found through their searching methods.

Figure 4-14 shows the page source for the United States Department of Labor home page. It displays the keywords, and the description used by their Web designer to describe the Web site. These keywords and description will help lead Internet users to this site, if they are looking for a related topic.

Figure 4-13 Meta tags in HTML

For searches that
use keywords

For searches that
use descriptions

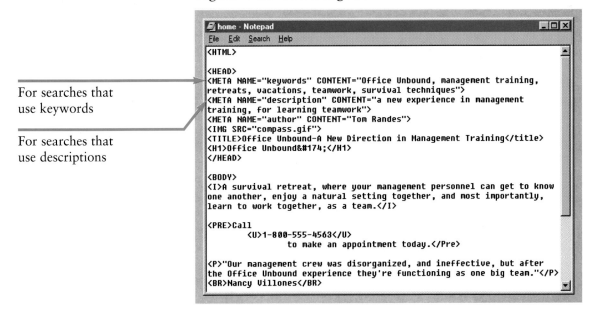

Figure 4-14 Page Source for Department of Labor home page

Keywords describing
Web page

A description of
the Web page

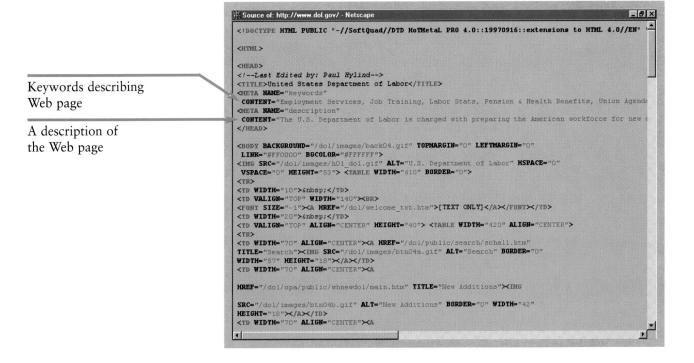

Add keywords and a description to the **Index** page. Also add yourself as the author to this page. Make sure the keywords and description appropriately describe this Web site.

It is a good idea to add misspelled words to your keywords. Sometimes users misspell words, and this will help them find your Web site anyway.

Publishing Web Pages

Concept

After you have added all of your objects, elements, and hyperlinks, formatted your text, added color, and refined your page layout to create an attractively spaced document, it is time to publish your site.

The first step is to organize your files. Create one folder for all your files. Place your HTML source documents in the folder. You can either put all your images in the same folder or create an images subfolder. These organizational tasks can be completed as you are creating your site, but you may find it easier to organize everything at the end.

There are several programs you can use to publish your Web site to an Internet Service Provider (ISP). You can use Fetch for Macintosh, or WS_FTP for Windows. Both of these programs will walk you through the process of uploading files.

Before you upload your Web pages you will need to contact the server to find out what their protocol is. They may want you to set a password to ensure that you are the only one who can upload files to a particular location. You will also need to get the URL for your ISP and find out what name they want you to assign to your home page. After you have this information, you can use an FTP program such as Fetch, or WS_FTP to transfer your files to the server.

If you used relative URLs, they will not change when you upload your files. As long as they are all in the same folder, the pathnames will not have to be adjusted. If you used absolute URLs, on the other hand, you will either have to change them to reflect the file's new location, or change them to relative URLs.

Figure 4-15 displays the NOAA home page, while Figure 4-16 shows you the HTML source of the NASA home page, as it is displayed in a browser. Both of these pages feature many of the Web page elements that you have learned about in this book.

Figure 4-15 NOAA home page displayed in a browser

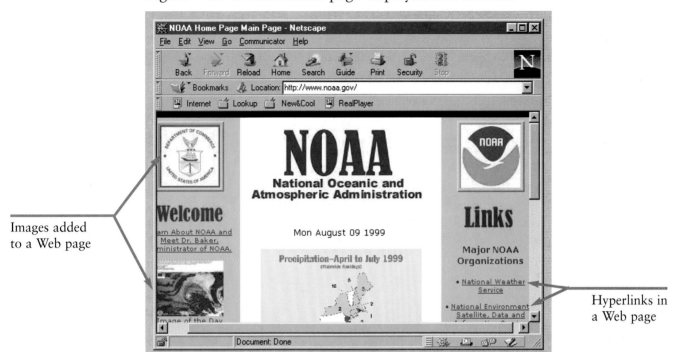

Images added to a Web page

Hyperlinks in a Web page

Figure 4-16 Page source for NASA home page

```
Source of: http://www.nasa.gov/ - Netscape
<HTML>
<HEAD>
<TITLE>NASA Homepage</TITLE>
</HEAD>

<BODY BACKGROUND="/images/bg_tile3.gif" BGCOLOR="#FFFFFF" TEXT="#000C

<TABLE WIDTH=600 BORDER=0 CELLPADDING=0 CELLSPACING=0>
<TR VALIGN=TOP>
<TD ALIGN=CENTER WIDTH=600>

        <TABLE WIDTH=590 BORDER=0 CELLPADDING=0 CELLSPACING=0>
        <TR VALIGN=TOP>
        <TD WIDTH=140>

                <TABLE WIDTH=140 BORDER=0 CELLPADDING=0 CELLSPACING=(
                <TR VALIGN=TOP>
                <TD WIDTH=140 align=center>
<A HREF="http://www.nasa.gov"><IMG align=center SRC="/images/hotnasa.
                </TD>
                </TR>
                <TR VALIGN=TOP>
                <TD WIDTH=140 ALIGN=CENTER>

<P><B><!--Today-->Aug 9, 1999<!--Today--></B>
                </TD>
```

A table in HTML

A table row in HTML

A hyperlink in HTML

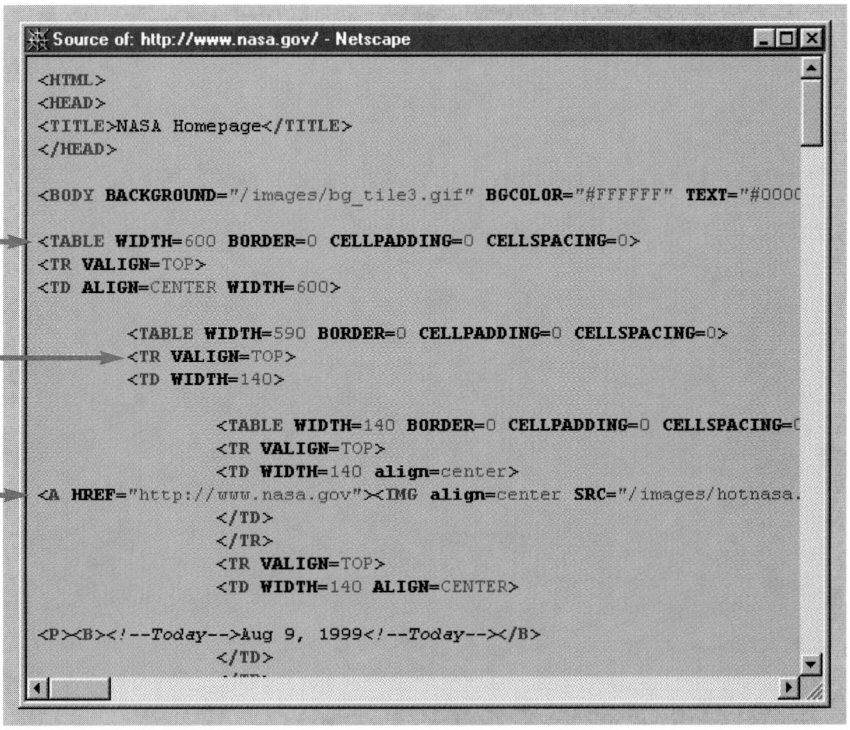

Shortcuts

Form Elements	Tags	Closing Tags
The contained elements are part of a form	<FORM>	</FORM>
Create a text box	<INPUT TYPE="TEXT">	
Create a large text box	<TEXTAREA>	</TEXTAREA>
Create a radio button	<INPUT TYPE="RADIO"	
Create a check box	<INPUT TYPE="CHECKBOX"	
Create a pull-down menu with the following options	<SELECT>	</SELECT>
Create a scroll box with the following options	<SELECT SIZE=N>	</SELECT>
Place the following option in a pull-down menu or a scroll box	<OPTION>	
Set default option	<OPTION SELECTED>	
Insert a submit button	<INPUT TYPE="SUBMIT"	
Insert a reset button	<INPUT TYPE="RESET"	

Identify Key Features

Name the items indicated by callouts in **Figure 4-17**

Figure 4-17 A form in an HTML document

```
form - Notepad
File  Edit  Search  Help
<P>City: <INPUT TYPE="TEXT" SIZE=28 NAME="city">
State: <INPUT TYPE="TEXT" SIZE=2 NAME="state">
Zip Code: <INPUT TYPE="TEXT" SIZE=5 NAME></P>

<P>Please choose a payment method:</P>
<INPUT TYPE="RADIO" NAME="payment" VALUE="credit">Credit
<INPUT TYPE="RADIO" NAME="payment" VALUE="debit">Debit
<INPUT TYPE="RADIO" NAME="payment" VALUE="check">Check

<P>You may check more than one:</P>
<P>Why would you like to attend Office Unbound?</P>
<INPUT TYPE="CHECKBOX" NAME="attend" VALUE="fun">Fun
<INPUT TYPE="CHECKBOX" NAME="attend" VALUE="learn">Learn survival
techniques
<INPUT TYPE="CHECKBOX" NAME="attend" VALUE="meet">Meet new people
<INPUT TYPE="CHECKBOX" NAME="attend" VALUE="know">Know my coworkers
better

<P>How long will you be staying?</P>
<SELECT NAME="staying">
<OPTION SELECTED VALUE="weekend">Weekend
<OPTION VALUE="3">3 Days
<OPTION VALUE="5">5 Days
<OPTION VALUE="7">1 Week
</SELECT>
```

Select The Best Answer

10. Input fields on a form are also known as

11. Text entry fields are also known as

12. Use this attribute to mark the default option in a pull-down menu

13. Without this button information cannot be collected from a form

14. The two methods for submitting a form are Post and

15. This tag adds elements to a Web page that are not visible when a page is displayed

16. To publish your Web pages you must submit them through an

17. Rather than displaying text, a password box usually displays

a. Selected

b. Get

c. ISP

d. Meta

e. Controls

f. Asterisks

g. Submit

h. Text boxes

HTML

Quiz (continued)

Complete the Statement

18. Tools that allow users to enter information onto a form are called:

    a. Boxes

    b. Form tools

    c. Input fields

    d. Entry parameters

19. The size value of a text entry field is measured in:

    a. Pixels

    b. Characters

    c. Inches

    d. Centimeters

20. Radio boxes and check boxes which have the same value for this attribute are considered a group:

    a. NAME

    b. SIZE

    c. OUTPUT

    d. VALUE

21. The size value for a scroll box designates:

    a. How many options you can select

    b. How many options are available

    c. How many options have the same value

    d. How many options are displayed on the Web page

22. Use this attribute to specify keywords or write a description of the Web page:

    a. TYPE

    b. ATTRIBUTE

    c. VALUE

    d. CONTENT

23. A more complicated way of collecting information from a form is using this type of script:

    a. Common Gateway Interface

    b. Common Form Interface

    c. Form Interface Script

    d. Script Gateway Form

24. A submit button will only work if:

    a. It has a value that accompanies it

    b. The Form tag specifies where the information will be sent

    c. The Input tag specifies where the information will be sent

    d. The Submit tag specifies where the information will be sent

25. To create a password text box, use this tag:

    a. <INPUT TYPE="PASSWORD">

    b. <PASSWORD SIZE=n>

    c. <PASSWORD NAME>

    d. <INPUT="PASSWORD">

Interactivity

Test Your Skills

1. Add a text entry field to a form:

    a. Create a new text document in Notepad.

    b. Create the basic HTML page structure.

    c. In the Body section of the document create a form.

    d. Within the form create two small text boxes, for first name and last name, and one large text box for address.

    e. Save the document as orders.

2. Add radio buttons and check boxes to a form:

    a. Add a group of three radio buttons and one check box to the orders form.

    b. The text to accompany the radio buttons is: How will you be paying for this order?. The radio button options are Credit, Debit, Check.

    c. The text for the check box is: Click here if this is a new account.

    d. Save the document as orders.

3. Create a pull-down menu on a form:

    a. Create a pull-down menu on the orders form.

    b. The text accompanying the menu is: Select the style you would like to purchase.

    c. The style options are: Alligator, Renegade, Maverick, Tidal, Coastal, Sonic, and Aero. The default selection is Tidal.

    d. Save the document as orders.

4. Collect information from a form:

    a. Add two push buttons, one submit button and one reset button to the bottom of the orders form.

    b. Add a Method attribute and Action attribute to the Form tag so that the information submitted is by Post, and sent to the e-mail address, info@sunglasscity.domain.com.

5. Help visitors find a page.

    a. Add a Meta tag with these keywords to the Head section of the orders form: orders, shopping, sunglasses, secure shopping, online shopping.

    b. Add this description and another Meta tag to the orders form: An online shipping experience designed to bring the latest fashions in sunglasses to you, the consumer.

    c. Save the document as orders.

Problem Solving

1. Great Work! You only have one more page to create for the Fixit Company, a form. First, create the HTML document in Notepad. Begin with the basic structure for every Web page. Then add the necessary input fields to enable efficient information gathering for the Fixit Company. They want the last name, first name, and middle initial for every visitor. Include controls for collecting the address, including an apartment # field. Next, collect credit card information, including expiration date. (Remember, some of these input fields may not vary greatly. Radio buttons or drop-down menus may facilitate data entry.) The company wants to identify its customers as private consumers, construction companies or hardware stores. It also wants to determine if they are first time customers, and if not, what method they used to buy products in the past. For example, were their purchases via the Internet, mail order, or from one of their stores? Choose appropriate controls and save the document as hardware.

2. Add some more controls to the hardware form you have been working on. Begin by creating a pull-down menu. The Fixit Company wants the menu to display options about the delivery process. Type: Choose a delivery option. The delivery options are: Next Day, Two day, within 5 days, within a week, or by special appointment. Once you have finished this menu you must create a scroll box. The scroll box will display who is going to pay the bill, i.e. who is being charged for the supplies. The options are: your company, the person who is having it delivered, a third party, or a third party company. Once you have finished creating the scroll box, add two buttons to the form. Add one submit button and one reset button. Make sure that the Form tag is written so that information from the form will be sent to the e-mail address info@fixit.domain.com. Save the document as hardware.

3. Open the fixit document. Create a link from the fixit page to the hardware page. Create three Meta tags. The first Meta tag should list the keywords: hardware, construction, supplies, personal tools, appliances, online supplies, online shopping, and secure shopping. Next, add a Meta tag with the company description: The Fixit Company, an online hardware store providing products to construction companies, hardware suppliers, and the private consumer. Finally, create a Meta tag that provides the author's name. Your name will be listed as the author's name. Save the document as fixit.

4. Open the Personal page you have been working on. Create a new page called guest. Make it a guest book where visitors can sign in. You can create several controls to elicit feedback from visitors. For example, you can collect their names, addresses, and telephone numbers, to compile a mailing list. If you are going to advertise your page, compiling the demographics of your visitors is a good idea. Find out their age, sex, and geographical area. Select appropriate controls and create Submit and Reset buttons. Construct the Form tag so that the information is submitted to your e-mail address. Create a hyperlink labeled Home, to connect the guest page to the personal page. Create another hyperlink labeled Guest book, to connect the personal page to the guest page. Format the guest page to complement the style and tone you set for the Web site. Save the file as guest, and test the Web site in several browsers. Verify that all the hyperlinks work and that your information is consistently presented. Complete any final formatting changes. If you already have an ISP, you are ready to follow their instructions and publish the site

Appendix A: Tag and Attribute Reference Guide

\<Tag\>/Attribute	*Function*
\<A\>	**Creates an anchor or link**
ACCESSKEY	Creates a keyboard shortcut to the link
HREF	Specifies the URL of the target
NAME	Marks an area on a page to jump to
\<AREA\>	**Specifies coordinates of an image map**
ACCESSKEY	Creates a keyboard shortcut to a hotspot
COORDS	Specifies the coordinates for a hotspot
HREF	Specifies the URL target of the hotspot
NOHREF	Creates hotspots with no target
SHAPE	Specifies the shape of the hotspot
\<B\>	**Displays text in bold**
\<BGSOUND\>	**Adds background sound to a page**
LOOP	Specifies how many times the sound should play
SRC	Specifies the location of the sound
\<BIG\>	**Makes text appear bigger**
\<BLINK\>	**Makes text disappear and reappear**
\<BLOCKQUOTE\>	**Contained text is blocked off separately from rest of text**
\<BODY\>	**Contained text makes up the Body section of the page**
ALINK	Specifies the color of an active link
LINK	Specifies the color of a new link
VLINK	Specifies the color of a visited link
BACKGROUND	Adds a background image to a page
BGCOLOR	Adds a background color to a page
TEXT	Specifies the color of text for the page
\<BR\>	**Creates a line break**
CLEAR	Stops a text wrap around the sides of an image
\<BUTTON\>	**Creates a button**
ACCESSKEY	Creates a keyboard shortcut for the button
NAME	Identifies the button
VALUE	Specifies the type of button to create
\<CAPTION\>	**Creates a caption for a table**
ALIGN	Aligns the caption above or below a table

Appendix A: (continued)

<Tag>/Attribute	*Function*
<CENTER>	Used to center images, text and other objects
<CITE>	Contained text is a citation or quotation
<CODE>	Contained text is computer code
<DD>	A definition in a list
<DL>	Creates a definition list
<DT>	Contained text is a definition term
<EM>	Emphasizes text

<EMBED>
  ALIGN
  AUTOSTART
  CONTROLS
  LOOP
  SRC
	Embeds multimedia files in a page
	Aligns controls
	Starts multimedia file automatically
	Displays play, pause, and rewind buttons
	Specifies how many times multimedia file should play
	Specifies the location of the multimedia file

<FONT>
  COLOR
  FACE
  SIZE
	Formats text on a Web page
	Specifies text color
	Specifies text font
	Specifies text size

<FORM>
  ACTION
  METHOD
	Creates a form
	Specifies where the information from a form will be sent
	Specifies the method of collecting information from a form

<HN> ALIGN	Creates a Header Aligns the Header
<HEAD>	Contained text is part of the Head section of the page
<HTML>	Contained text is written in HTML
<I>	Italicizes text

Appendix A: (continued)

<Tag>/Attribute	Function
\<IMG\>	**Inserts an image**
ALIGN	Aligns the image
ALT	Displays text if image is unavailable
BORDER	Adds a border to an image
CONTROLS	Adds video controls to a multimedia file
LOOP	Specifies how many times a video should run
SRC	Specifies the location of an image
START	Specifies when a video should start
USEMAP	Specifies what image map is being used
\<INPUT\>	**Creates an entry field or control on a form**
ACCESSKEY	Creates a keyboard shortcut to a form object
CHECKED	Makes a radio button or check box selected by default
DISABLED	Disable a form object
MAXLENGTH	Specifies maximum characters allowed to be entered
NAME	Identifies the data collected by a form
SIZE	Specifies the size of text boxes
SRC	Specifies the location of an image
TYPE	Determining type of entry field or control to be added
VALUE	Specifies value of options on a form
\<KBD\>	**Specifies keyboard text**
\<LI\>	**Contained text is a list item**
TYPE	Specifies the symbols used to mark each list item
VALUE	Specifies value of a list item
\<MAP\>	**Creates an image map**
NAME	Names an image map so it can be referred to later
\<MARQUEE\>	**Creates moving text**
BEHAVIOR	Specifies how the text moves, slides, scrolls, alternates
DIRECTION	Specifies the direction in which the text moves
LOOP	Specifies how many times the text repeats
\<META\>	**Specifies information about a Web page**
NAME	Specifies the type of information being described
CONTENT	Describes the Web page
\<OL\>	**Creates an ordered list**
TYPE	Specifies symbols to mark each list item
START	Specifies value for each list item
\<OPTION\>	**Creates a group of options in a form**
SELECTED	Specifies the default option
VALUE	Specifies values of menu options

Appendix A: (continued)

\<Tag\>/Attribute	*Function*

\<P\>
    ALIGN
	Creates a new paragraph
	    Aligns the paragraph

\<PRE\>	Displays text exactly as it appears in HTML document
\<Q\>	Contained text is quoted
\<S\>	Displays text with a line through it, same as \<STRIKE\>
\<SAMP\>	Displays text in a monospaced font

\<SELECT\>
    NAME
    MULTIPLE
    SIZE
	Creates a menu in a form
	    Identifies data collected in form
	    Allows the user to select multiple options
	    Specifies the size of the menu, visible on the screen

\<SMALL\>	Makes text appear smaller
\<STRIKE\>	Displays text with a line through it, same as \<S\>
\<STRONG\>	Emphasizes text
\<SUB\>	Displays text as subscript
\<SUP\>	Displays text as superscript

\<TABLE\>
    BGCOLOR
    BORDER
    BORDERCOLOR
    CELLPADDING
 	
    CELLSPACING
	Creates a table
	    Specifies the background color of a table
	    Specifies the thickness of the border
	    Specifies the color of the border
	    Specifies the amount of space between a cells' contents, and border
	    Specifies the amount of space between cells

\<TD\>
    ALIGN
    BGCOLOR
    ROWSPAN
	Creates a table cell
	    Aligns contents within a cell
	    Specifies the background color of a cell
	    Specifies how many rows a cell should use

\<TEXTAREA\>
    ACCESSKEY
    NAME
    ROWS
    COLS
	Creates a large text box
	    Creates a keyboard shortcut to the text box
	    Identifies the data collected from the form
	    Specifies the number of rows in the text box
	    Specifies the number of columns in the text box

Appendix A: (continued)

<Tag>/Attribute	Function
<TH> ALIGN BGCOLOR ROWSPAN	Creates a Header in a table Aligns the Header in a cell Specifies the background color in the Headers' cell Specifies how many rows the Header should use
<TITLE>	Creates the title in the Title bar area
<TR> ALIGN BGCOLOR	Creates a row in a table Aligns the data in a row Specifies the background color for a row
<TT>	Displays monospaced font
<U>	Underlines contained text
<UL>	Creates an unordered list
<VAR>	Displays variable text

Appendix B: Special Character Codes

Character	Code	Character	Code
À	À or À	Ì	Ì or Ì
Á	Á or Á	Í	Í or Í
Â	Â or Â	Î	Î or Î
Ã	Ã or Ã	Ï	Ï or Ï
Ä	Ä or Ä	ì	ì or ì
Å	Å or Å	í	í or í
Æ	Æ or Æ	î	î or î
à	à or à	ï	ï or ï
á	á or á	Ò	Ò or Ò
â	â or â	Ó	Ó or Ó
ã	ã or ã	Ô	Ô or Ô
ä	ä or ä	Õ	Õ or Õ
å	å or å	Ö	Ö or Ö
æ	æ or æ	Ø	Ø or Ø
È	È or È	Œ	&#140;
É	É or É	ò	ò or ò
Ê	Ê or Ê	ó	ó or ó
Ë	Ë or Ë	ô	ô or ô
è	è or è	õ	õ or õ
é	é or é	ö	ö or &ouml
ê	ê or ê	ø	ø or &oslash
ë	ë or ë	œ	&#156;

Appendix B: (continued)

Character	Code	Character	Code
Ù	Ù or Ù	@	&#64;
Ú	Ú or Ú	~	&#126;
Û	Û or Û	ƒ	&#131;
Ü	Ü or Ü	…	&#133;
ù	ù or ù	†	&#134;
ú	ú or ú	‡	&#135;
û	û or û	‰	&#137;
ü	ü or ü	•	&#149;
Ÿ	&#159;	™	™ or ™
ÿ	ÿ or &yuml	¡	¡ or ¡
Ç	Ç or Ç	¢	¢ or ¢
ç	ç or ç	£	£ or £
ß	ß or ß	¥	¥ or ¥
Ñ	Ñ or Ñ	§	§ or §
ñ	ñ or ñ	¨	¨ or ¨
!	&#33;	©	© or ©
"	&#34;	«	« or «
#	&#35;	®	® or ®
$	&#36;	°	° or °
%	&#37;	±	± or ±
&	& or &	`	&#96;
*	&#42;	´	´ or &acute

Appendix B: (continued)

Character	Code
µ	µ or µ
¶	¶ or ¶
·	· or ·
ª	ª or ª
º	º or º
»	» or »
¼	¼ or ¼
½	½ or ½
¾	¾ or ¾
¿	¿ or ¿
∂	ð or ð
<	<
>	>

Appendix C: A Guide to the Sixteen Predefined Colors

Name	Color
Black	
Silver	
Gray	
Purple	
Navy	
Blue	
Cyan	
Maroon	
Red	
Magenta	
Olive	
Green	
Lime	
Teal	
Yellow	
White	

Appendix D: Reference Guide to Hexadecimal Color Values

Hexadecimal Code	Color
#7FFFD4	
#8A2BE2	
#5F9EA0	
#008B8B	
#483D8B	
#00BFFF	
#00CED1	
#1E90FF	
#ADD8E6	
#B0C4DE	
#E0FFFF	
#66CDAA	
#0000CD	
#191970	
#B0E0E6	
#87CEEB	

Appendix D: (continued)

Hexadecimal Code	Color
#7FFF00	
#006400	
#556B2F	
#8FBC8F	
#228B22	
#ADFF2F	
#7CFC00	
#90EE90	
#32CD32	
#3CB371	
#00FA9A	
#F5FFFA	
#98FB98	
#2E8B57	
#00FF7F	

Appendix D: (continued)

Hexadecimal Code	Color
#FF7F50	
#DC1436	
#8B008B	
#8B0000	
#E9967A	
#FF1493	
#B22222	
#FF69B4	
#CD5C5C	
#FFB6C1	
#FFA07A	
#FFE4E1	
#FFA500	
#BC8F8F	
#FA8072	

Appendix D: (continued)

Hexadecimal Code	Color
#FFF8DC	
#B8860B	
#FFD700	
#DAA520	
#F0E68C	
#FFFACD	
#EEE8AA	
#FFEFD5	
#D2B48C	
#F4A460	
#8B4513	
#BDB76B	
#D2691E	
#DEB887	
#A52A2A	

Appendix D: (continued)

Hexadecimal Code	Color
#9400D3	
#E6E6FA	
#FFF0F5	
#9370DB	
#C71585	
#DA70D6	
#DB7093	
#DDA0DD	
#EE82EE	
#BA55D3	
#9932CC	
#640537	
#ED9DCA	
#FD00CB	

Appendix D: (continued)

Hexadecimal Code	Color
#FAEBD7	
#F0FFFF	
#F5F5DC	
#FFE4C4	
#FFEBCD	
#FFFAF0	
#DCDCDC	
#F8F8FF	
#FFFFF0	
#FAF0E6	
#FFE4B5	
#FFDEAD	
#FDF5E6	
#FFDAB9	
#FFF5EE	
#F5F5F5	

Appendix D: (continued)

Hexadecimal Code	Color
#F5DEB3	
#FFFAFA	
#708090	
#778899	
#DCDCDC	
#696969	
#2F4F4F	
#A9A9A9	
#A1A1A1	
#404040	
#212121	

A

Absolute pathname
A method of naming the location of objects and images, by describing the direct path to get there including listing all of the folders that need to be opened.

Action
An attribute that tells a browser where to send the information from a form, it can be mailed to an e-mail address or sent to a Web page, which has a CGI script.

Adobe PageMill
An HTML editor that allows you to create Web pages graphically while the program writes the HTML for you.

Adobe Photoshop
An image editing program which can be used to find the RGB content of colors, used for Hexadecimal values, or used to locate pixel coordinates to create an image map.

Align
An attribute that moves any object, including text, to the left , right, or center of a page.

Anchors
A way of marking objects or text so that a link may be created that connects a user to the location of the anchor.

Angle brackets
These are symbols created by using your keyboard, all tags, attributes, and values are written within angle brackets.

Area tag
A tag that allows you to specify the pixel coordinates of an image map, or hot spot.

Attributes
Used with tags and values, attributes are used to describe the way an object should be displayed by a browser.

B

Background color
The color that appears on the background on a Web page, specified by the Hexadecimal values of colors.

Background sound
Sound that can be added to a Web page, so that the sound will be heard whenever a Web page is opened.

Backspace key
A key on keyboards that allows users to delete text that appears on the page in Notepad.

Big
A physical character tag that makes text appear larger.

Body
A tag that specifies to browsers that the contained text is part of the Web page, this section makes up most of the Web page.

Bold
A physical character tag that instructs a browser to display text in bold.

Border
Lines that can be added to, and surround images and tables, the thickness and color of borders may be specified with certain attributes.

Browser
See Web Browser.

Bulleted list
A list that does not have a specific order so the list items are marked with bullets rather than numbers or letters, this is the same as an Unordered list.

C

Cell
The empty spaces that are created by the rows and columns of a table. Contains the information in a table.

Character tag
A type of tag that tells a browser to display text a certain way, there are two types of character tags: physical and logical.

Check box
A check box is another way of answering a yes or no question, the user has an option of checking the box to select it, a yes answer, or not checking it, a no answer. Check boxes may also be used in place of radio buttons.

Circle
A value used with the Shape attribute to specify the shape of a hotspot on an image map, specified in x, y, r coordinates.

Clear
An attribute used with the line break tag that stops a text wrap at a specified location.

Click
To press and release a mouse button in one motion; usually refers to the left mouse button.

Code
A logical character tag that tells a browser to display the text as computer code.

Column
The vertical border of a table, that intersects with the rows to make up the empty spaces of the table called cells.

Common Gateway Interface (CGI)
A programming language used to create scripts that are used to extract information collected from a form.

Coordinates
Used to specify the exact location of a hotspot on an image map, by using the x, y location of pixels on an image.

Control
An object that makes data entry easier and more efficient, most controls appear on form pages, such as check boxes, and radio buttons.

D

Desktop
The standard Microsoft Windows screen, it is designed to have the appearance of an actual desktop.

Definition list
A list that includes a descrption for each term, the type of list one might find in a dictionary, or glossary of terms.

Dialog Box
A box that groups functions together, it performs certain actions depending on the commands you use and the options you select.

Drop-Down Menu
see pull-down menu.

E

EM tag
A logical character tag that instructs a browser to emphasize the contained text, usually emphasized in bold.

E-mail link
A hyperlink that opens a browsers mail program with an e-mail address specified so the user can send e-mail to the specified location.

Embed tag
A tag used to to embed multimedia files on a Web page, it works with a Netscape plug-in that allows users to control the way multimedia files are displayed.

F

Fetch
A program for Macintosh computers that moves files from your computer to a location provided by an ISP.

File
A menu on the menu bar, it provides commands that have to do with saving, opening, printing, storing, and performing other filing options on your HTML pages.

Font
The style in which text appears. Bold, italic, script, serif, and sans serif are all styles associated with different fonts.

Font tag
The tag that makes formatting changes to text, you can use this tag to affect size, color, and other formatting options.

Form page
A type of Web page that asks the user for information, once the information has been entered the page may be sent to the Web manager, and saved, to a page with a CGI script, or sent to an e-mail address so the data can be recorded.

Form tag
The tag that specifies that the contained text is to be included with the form, and how the data will be collected when the form is submitted.

Formatting
The process of adding elements to your Web page, including objects, text, colors, and other important Web components to give your pages a certain look or style, and make it attractive.

G

Graphics
Another term used to describe images that appear on a Web page.

Graphic Interchange Format (GIF)
A format in which images are saved, where the image is compressed so that it does not take up much space, and doesn't take long to download.

Hypertext Markup Language (HTML)
A code used for designing Web pages. FrontPage writes HTML code for you, but a knowledgable user may also write HTML code for a page in FrontPage.

H

Head
A tag that specifies that all contained text will appear in the head section of the Web page.

Headers
Tags used to format text so that they will appear in one of six Header formats used to mark sections on a Web page.

Hexadecimal color values
A way of coding colors so that they can be specified on a Web page. The format is #RRGGBB, and based on the RGB, or Red Green and Blue content of the color.

Home page
The first page that a visitor sees when they enter your Web site. It is where they begin to navigate through the site.

Hotspot
Another name for an image map, when an image is formatted so that a particular spot on the image is linked to a target page. When clicked the hotspot acts as a hyperlink.

HREF
The attribute that specifies the URL of the target page that the hyperlink will link to. The URL cab be relative or absolute.

Hyperlink
A hyperlink is a piece of text that links to another Web page.

I

I-beam
When you move the mouse pointer over text or an area of a page where text may be inserted it turns into an I-beam so named because it looks like an I-beam.

Icon
A small graphic that identifies an object.

Image Edit
An image editing program that may be used to identify the pixel coordinates of an image so that they may be used to create an image map.

Image map
An image that is formatted so that a particular spot on the image is linked to a target page. When clicked the spot acts as a hyperlink.

Image tag
The tag that is used to format and insert an image, there is no closing tag required for this tag.

Inline image
An image that appears with a Web page when it is opened in a browser, it does not have to be downloaded.

Input field
Another name for a control on a form. Input fields are used to collect data from a user in the form of text boxes, radio buttons, check boxes, etc.

Input tag
The tag that adds an input field to a form, used with the Type attribute it specifies the type of input field that will be added to a form.

Insertion point
A flashing point on a page, it marks the point where text will be entered on the page.

Internet
A global network of computers exchanging information over the network, it includes the Web servers, the individual user, and organizations that manage the networks.

Internet Explorer
A Web browser create by Microsoft, one of the most popular browsers used to search the Internet.

Internet Service Provider (ISP)
An Internet service provider is simply a company that manages locations and files on the Internet, so that you can publish pages, and search the Internet.

Italics
A physical character tag that tells a browser to display the contained text in italics.

J

Joint Photographic Experts Group (JPEG)
A format in which images are saved, where the image is compressed so that it does not take up much space, and doesn't take long to download.

K

Keyboard shortcut
A way of interacting with objects on a Web page using the keyboard with shortcuts that were programmed into a Web page.

Keywords
The attribute used with the Meta tag used to describe a Web page so that visitors will be able to find your page.

L

Line break
A tag used to create spacing in a Web page, the spacing between line breaks is less than with paragraphs.

List
A list is a way of organizing information on a Web page by displaying it in list format.

List item
A tag that allows you to add more items to a list.

Logical character tag
A character tag that tells a browser to perform a certain function on text, it does not specify exactly how the browser should perform this action.

M

Macromedia Dreamweaver
An HTML editor that allows you to create Web pages graphically while the program writes the HTML for you.

Map tag

The tag that is used to create an image map, it specifies the image to use, which is referenced using the Usemap attribute.

Menu

A list of related commands.

Menu bar

Found below the Title bar, it contains the names of menus that present lists of commands to choose from.

Meta tag

A tag used to describe your Web pages so that search engines and users searching the Internet will be able to locate your Web page.

Method

An attribute that describes the way data will be collected from a form, the two methods are Post and Get.

Microsoft FrontPage

A graphical HTML editor that adds objects to Web pages for you, and writes the HTML code.

Mouse pointer

The arrow shaped cursor on the screen that you control by guiding the mouse on your desk. The shape of the mouse pointer can change depending on the task being executed.

Multimedia file

Files that are added to a Web page that do more than still images and graphics. Sound, video, and animation are examples of multimedia files.

N

Nested list

A list in which each list item contains another list within it, the second list is nested within the first.

Netscape Navigator

A Web browser create by Netscape, one of the most popular browsers used to search the Internet.

Notepad

A text editor program found on Windows, used to write and edit text, may be used to create HTML dcouments.

Numbered list

A list whose list items are arranged in a specific order so they are marked by numbers or letters, his is the same as an Ordered list.

O

Option tag

A tag used to create an group of options on a form in the format of a pull-down menu.

Ordered list

A type of list in which the the list items are ordered by marking them with numbers, letters, or roman numerals.

P

Page Setup

A dialog box that allows you to set printing options for printing documents, it is accessible from the File menu.

Paint Shop Pro

An image editing program that allows you to locate pixel coordinates on an image in order to specify the coordinates on an image map.

Paragraph tag

A tag that creates spaces on a Web page, these spaces are greater than the spaces created by line breaks.

Password

An input type that creates a password text box that displays asterisks or bullets rather than the text the user is typing.

Pathname

A way of specifying the locations of pages and objects, there are two ways of specifying pathnames, relative and absolute.

Physical character tag

A character tag that instructs a browser exactly how to display the text.

Pico

A text editor program for Unix systems that allows you to write and edit text, and create HTML documents.

Pixels

Locations on an image, specified in x, y coordinates that are used to specify the location and size of hotspots on image maps.

Polygon

A value which specifies that shape of a hotspot on an image map, it is specified in x, y, x, y, x, y coordinates.

Preformatted text

Text that is contained within tags that instruct the browser to display it exactly as it appears in the HTML document.

Print

A command found on the File menu that allows you to print a copy of the Notepad screen, so that you can have a hard copy of the document you are working on.

Properties

A button available on the Print dialog box that allows you to select the print options available.

Pull-down menu

Controls that are added to a form, they only display one option, but if you click a down arrow a menu appears with more options.

Push button

A button that is added to a form page that allows a user to submit a form or to reset a form, these options may be set when the button is created.

R

Radio button

A group of buttons that allows the user to select one or more of several options. Users may be allowed to select more than one, or can be limited to only one selection, out of several radio buttons.

Rectangle

A value that is used with the Shape attribute to specify the shape of a hotspot on an image map, specified with x, y, x, y coordinates.

Relative pathname

A pathname that specifies the name of a file but not the exact location, this is useful if all of the files are located in the same folder.

Reset button
> A push button added to a form that allows the user to reset the form, and clear all the information from the input fields.

Row
> The horizontal border of a table, it intersects with columns to create the empty spaces called cells.

S

Save
> A command found on the File menu that saves a file simply by overwriting the existing saved document.

Save As
> A command found on the File menu that allows you to save a file with a new name and a new location.

Scroll box
> A control added to a form that displays several options at once, and allows the user to scroll through the menu of available options.

Size
> An attribute used with several different tags that allows the user to specify the size of objects and text.

Small tag
> A physical character tag that tells a browser to display the text in a smaller font.

Source
> An attribute that uses pathnames to specify the location of an image or a multimedia file so it can be displayed on a Web page.

Special characters
> Characters and symbols that do not appear on a keyboard that can be inserted onto a Web page by using special codes.

Strong tag
> A logical character tag that tells a browser to emphasize the contained text.

Submit button
> A push button added to a form that allows the user to send the data filled out on a form to the specified location.

T

Table
> An object that you can insert into a Web page to help organize information. The table is made up of rows and columns which create cells, the cells contain the information.

Table header
> A tag that allows you to add a cell with a Header, these Headers are useful for organizing information in a table.

Table row
> A tag that creates a new row of cells in a table, you can add as many rows as neccessary to a table.

Tags
> Commands written in HTML that instruct a browser how to display objects and text that are specified, and contained within the tags.

Target
> The page, or location that a hyperlink links to. When creating a hyperlink the target page or URL must be specified. The target page must also be in working order for the hyperlink to work.

TeachText
> A text editor program that allows you to write and edit text, and is used to create HTML documents.

Text box
> see Text entry field.

Text editor
> A simple word processing program that allows you to write and edit text, and allows you to create HTML documents.

Text entry field
> Controls that are added to a form that allow the user to enter data into a text box, whose size is specified.

Title
> A tag that creates a title for your page, this title will appear in the title bar of a browser whenever your Web page is opened.

Title bar
> The bar that appears at the top of the browser window, it displays the title of the page that is specified in the HTML document that is being displayed.

U

Underline
> A physical character tag that instructs the browser to display the contained text underlined.

Uniform Resource Location (URL)
> The address of a Web page. Every page has its own URL, no two URL's are exactly the same.

Unordered list
> A list that does not have a specific order, so the list items are marked by bullets rather than numbers or letters.

Usemap
> An attribute that allows you to specify the image you would like to use to create an image map from, the image map is referenced with the Map tag.

V

Values
> Specify how an attribute will affect the Web page by specifying how the browser should display it.

W

Web Browser
> A program that has the abiltity to display Web pages, and can access them off of the Internet, it displays pages by reading the code they are written in.

Web Page
> A document that appears on the Internet with its own URL. It may contain graphics, text, or any number of elements that may be viewed once it is published.

Web Server
> A computer running software that stores Web pages and objects, so that when a browser requests a page or object, the server furnishes the request, the browser interprets the objects as pages, text, graphics, etc.

Web site
> One or more Web pages that are linked and may be navigated by a visitor. Web sites are managed and owned by a person, company, or an organization.

Windows Taskbar
> Usually located at the bottom of your desktop screen, it contains buttons that allow you to open programs and perform certain functions.

Wordpad

A text editor program that allows you to write and edit text, and allows you to create HTML documents.

Wrapping text

A method of designing Web pages so that when an image inserted, the text is displayed next to the image, for as far down as the image goes on the page.

WS_FTP

A program used with Windows that moves your files from a computer to an ISP so you can publish and update Web pages.

Index